JULIAN OF NORWICH

A Revelation of Love

JULIAN OF NORWICH

A Revelation of Love

Newly translated from Middle English

by

JOHN SKINNER

ARTHUR JAMES

EVESHAM

FOR JUDITH

wife and friend, companion in Life

First published in 1996 by

ARTHUR JAMES LTD
4 Broadway Road
Evesham
Worcestershire WR11 6BH

© John Skinner 1996

A catalogue record for this book is available
from the British Library.

ISBN 0 85305 355 3

Typeset in Monotype Joanna by
Strathmore Publishing Services, London N7

Printed in Great Britain by
The Guernsey Press Company Ltd, Guernsey, C.I.

Preface

'I HAVE been reading Lady Julian of Norwich,' declares C. S. Lewis in a letter to his former pupil, the Benedictine mystic Bede Griffiths. 'A dangerous book, clearly: I'm glad I didn't read it much earlier.' Thomas Merton wrote simply: 'There can be no doubt that Lady Julian is the greatest of the English mystics.'

So who was this powerful Lady Julian? She was careful to conceal any personal details of her life except those that bore directly upon the authenticity of her experience of the Showings. Thus we do not even know her name; yet we do know the exact date of her *Revelation* – 8 May 1373 – and, indirectly, her date of birth, somewhere in December 1342. And while there is no date for her death, she herself tells us that for twenty years following the Showings she dwelt upon their meaning. We also have records of Norwich wills, one of which bequeaths to Dame Julian, still living in 1428, making her a very old lady in her late eighties; but we cannot be certain that this is the same as the author of *A Revelation*.

Anchorites were a common part of medieval life. Henry V would consult the hermit of Westminster Abbey at critical moments in his reign. In Norwich, they were particularly numerous, owing in part perhaps to the wealth of the city and the ready support given by its citizens to such holy men and women. The role they fulfilled was not merely spiritual, their prayers and counsels benefiting the community at large; sometimes they also performed practical functions. Richard Ferneys, for instance, was the hermit of Newbridge; as well as saying his prayers, his duties included repair and upkeep of the bridge across the Wensum. Others would occupy themselves in mending roads or some other such public service.

Before becoming an anchorite, candidates had to convince

their bishop or religious superior that they had a genuine calling to the life; evidence was also required that they were materially provided for. Once they had passed this scrutiny, they were then formally immured in their anchorhold and subject to a strict way of life that in most cases meant they would remain hermits until their death. However, not all took a formal vow of this nature, as recommended in the *Ancrene Riwle*. This treatise, written for the guidance and discipline of would-be anchorites, affords an insight into their way of life.

They would have had two servants to care for them, not so much a luxury as a necessary buffer against intrusion from the outside world. In Julian's case, we know these would have been women; Richard Ferneys, another recluse living in Norwich, on the other hand had a boy as well as a woman servant, whom he called his *custodes*, or, as we might say today, keepers. The anchorite would certainly be single and vow to lead a chaste life. Those who were already religious, such as the Carmelite Thomas Scrope, another of Julian's contemporaries, were simply licensed to become hermits within their community; others again were admitted as lay anchorites to live within a friary or convent.

In Julian's case, she took up her living in an anchor cell – a generous two-roomed dwelling – propped against the walls of St Julian in Conesford Street. The little church was one of the humblest in the whole city, its squat round tower housing perhaps a single Angelus bell. Here she would have attended each morning, peering through her leper's squint window to the altar where the priest prayed the dawn mass. She would have received the Eucharist only rarely, perhaps once a month. Outside visitors would also have been restricted. (The *Ancrene Riwle* warns against such occasions of useless chatter and dissipation.) But we know, from her own account, that Margery Kempe visited Julian and stayed on for several days. She was particularly anxious to obtain Julian's approval for the 'very many holy speeches and converse with our Lord ... also the many wonderful revelations, which she described to the anchoress to find out if there were any deception in them. For the anchoress was an expert in such things and could give good advice.'

Here we have rare, first-hand evidence of Julian's reputation as a holy and wise woman. Admittedly, Margery Kempe was a great seeker of such reassurances. On this same visitation to Norwich, she tells of her meeting with the saintly Richard Caistor, priest of St Stephen's. She greeted the vicar at noon and asked if she might detain him for an hour or more that same afternoon in order to speak of the love of God. 'He, lifting up his hands and blessing himself, asked how any woman could occupy one or two hours with the love of our Lord. "I shan't eat a thing till I find out."' Margery seems not to have been disconcerted by Caistor's response; her very innocence abroad enables her to report the experience.

And there is no doubting the sincerity of esteem in which she held Dame Julian, as she names her. And indeed the reply she received shows the classic hallmarks of someone well practised in advice of the soul. Julian bade her, reports Margery in her Book (dictated to a cleric, since she herself could neither read nor write), remain obedient to God's will and to fulfil with all her strength whatever he might put into her soul – provided it were not against the worship of God and the profit of her even Christians. For 'the Holy Ghost never urges a thing against charity, for if he did, he would be contrary to his own self, for he is all charity.'

It is hard not to smile at this unlikely encounter between Margery, the ebullient, much-travelled seeker after sanctity, and Julian, the quiet recluse, patiently preparing her own detailed account of God's dealings with her.

Before exploring Julian's writings, it is relevant to recall the background from which they emerged. The tradition of English mysticism was at its height in the late fourteenth century. Richard Rolle (c. 1290–1349) had written extensively, even poetically, of his mystical experiences and his Incendium Amoris or Fire of Love would almost certainly have been known to Julian.

The Augustinian, Walter Hilton (died 1395–6), was an exact contemporary, but by far and away the most influential and profound spiritual treatise of her day – if we are to exclude Julian's own book – is *The Cloud of Unknowing*. The authorship is unknown, but six other works are traditionally ascribed to the same hand.

It has often been asked how the fourteenth century came to welcome this flowering of mysticism and why England proved its focal point of expression. Such historical questions would remain rhetorical were it not for the emergence of the English language in that same season (when Chaucer too was to find his tongue), along with the rise of individual expression of political as well as religious ideas – as enunciated by the Lollards. This anti-establishment movement begun by John Wycliff was by Julian's day rapidly gaining ground, more especially in Norfolk. The church authority was not slow to respond. The Carmelite Thomas Netter (who was later to attend the burning of John Huss at the Council of Constance) was an active pursuivant and had already written an extensive tome that detailed Wycliff's every deviation from orthodoxy. This *Fasciculi Zizaniorum, Bundle of Tares*, he sent promptly to the pope, warning him of noxious seeds being sown in the Church's fields at large. There is no doubt that should *A Revelation* have fallen into his hands, with its original and provocatively forthright utterances on God's saving work, Thomas Netter would have made Julian answer personally for many of her sentences. C. S. Lewis found her dangerous: Netter would have condemned her out of hand.

Which brings us back to Merton's verdict: 'the greatest of the English mystics'. Let us first be clear what is a mystic. We can define such a person as having heightened perception of God and receiving thereby direct tangible communication from him. It is my belief that we ought not to set the mystic apart from ourselves, as somebody peculiar or star-struck. Rather is there a mystic in us all, if only we will attend. Certainly that is how Julian felt: all our common calling in this life is to come to know God and experience the touchings of his love.

Julian herself tells us that she experienced her Showings in three ways: first, bodily visions, that is to say she was aware of them with her senses – both sight and hearing and sometimes even smell; secondly, ghostly visions, by which she means spiritual visions and sayings directly imparted to her soul; and thirdly, intellectual enlightenment, whereby her mind was illumined with new understanding of God.

These are the three classical ways by which the mystic has always experienced God directly. The remarkable characteristic of Julian is that having undergone dramatic experiences of this nature, she is content to fall back upon the life of faithful prayer and patient practice of religious exercise more familiar to the rest of us.

It is common for the mystic to feel compelled to communicate something of their experience. In Julian's case, we feel as if the compulsion came from the very nature of that experience: that having known the love of God – for all his creation – she needed to share it abroad. This sense of the urgency of her message can be felt again and again in the manner in which Julian writes. At once, she is crying to get her words across and, at the exact moment, these very words break and splinter at the sheer burden she wishes them to bear. As Thomas Merton witnesses, no one has uttered more finely in the English tongue.

* * *

The scholar knows the writings of Julian of Norwich by their MSS numbers: namely, Sloane 2499 and 3705 in the British Library, and Fonds Anglais 40 in Paris Bibliothèque Nationale. Other partial renderings of Julian exist, plus the first printed edition by Cressey in 1670. But none of these pre-date the seventeenth century. The survival of our present text might therefore appear to rest upon a knife edge; no surprise, given the upheavals of the Henrician revolution that occurred barely a century or more after Julian's death. Its survival may appear as a slender chance, since we have but three MSS work upon, and these distanced from their original author by three hundred years. Yet the opposite is true: it is a tribute to the popularity, at the very least to the manner in which her book was regarded, that we have three such complete copies.

Yet we have a fourth, known as Add. 37790 (again in the British Library), which dates to the mid-fifteenth century. In nineteenth-century binding, yet written in the same hand, it draws together a number of writings of the English mystics, including Hilton's *Mirror of Simple Souls*. Included in this selection is what at first seemed a truncated text of Julian's *Revelation*. Like Margery Kempe's book, which turned up in an old Catholic library in the 1930s, this unique volume only came to light earlier this century. When scholars had deliberated, it was agreed that here was the only known example of Julian's first attempt at recording her Showings. Far from being a digest, this was a first draft of what was later to become the expanded Long Text that we know today.

In addition, this same document carries a clue as to the possible generation of copyists whose careful scripting (Julian predeceased Caxton by almost exactly a hundred years) enables us to read Julian today. In the margin on folio [page] 33 is a monogram that reads 'JG'. This is James Grenehalgh, a scribe who worked for the Carthusians at Sheen. He may indeed have become a Carthusian, but the important link is established spanning back to Julian's own original writing. This same link came under even more pressure with the dissolution of the monasteries and the destruction of much irreplaceable material. But dispersal was also another escape route. And it is presumably to the presence of English Catholic religious communities in exile on the Continent that we owe the survival of the Paris MS of Julian's writings.

The present translation is based upon the acknowledged critical edition of *A Revelation of Love* by Dr Marion Glasscoe (published by Exeter University). I would like to thank her for her great kindness and encouragement.

Revelations to one who could not read a letter, Anno Domini 1373

1

THIS first chapter tells in particular of the number of the revelations. This is a revelation of love that Jesus Christ, our endless bliss,* made in sixteen showings or revelations particular; of which the FIRST is the precious crowning of our Lord with thorns; it includes a showing of the Trinity with the Incarnation and tells of the unity between God and the soul; with many other fair showings of endless wisdom and teaching of love, in which all the showings that follow are grounded and oned.

The SECOND is the discolouring of his fair face, tokening of his most dear passion.

The THIRD is that our Lord God, all-mighty wisdom, all love, right as truly as he made every thing that is, also truly he does and works all thing that is done.

The FOURTH is the scourging of his tender body with plenteous shedding of his blood.

The FIFTH is that the fiend is overcome by the precious passion of Christ.

The SIXTH is the worshipful*[1] thanking by our Lord God in which he rewards all his blessed servants in heaven.

The SEVENTH is our often feeling of weal and of woe* – feeling well in ourselves when we are touched and fed by grace with true sureness of endless joy: the feeling of woe is temptation to be weighed down and irked by our fleshly living – with spiritual understanding that we are also surely kept in love, in woe as in weal, by the goodness of God.

---

* Words marked with an asterisk appear in the Glossary.

[1] worshipful: Julian uses this word in various shades of meaning, here to emphasize her reverence at God's intimate and continual dealings with us.

The EIGHTH is the last pains of Christ and his cruel dying.

The NINTH is how the blessed Trinity gladly consents to the hard passion of Christ and to his painful dying. In which joy and glad consent he wants us to be solaced and take heart with him until the time we shall come into fulfilment in heaven.

The TENTH is our Lord showing his love: how he rejoices to show us his blessed* heart broken in two.

The ELEVENTH is a high and spiritual showing of his most dear Mother.

The TWELFTH is that our Lord is the most worthy Being.

The THIRTEENTH is that our Lord God wishes us to attend carefully to all that he has done: the noble manner in which he makes all things; the excellence by which he made humankind to be above all his works; the precious satisfaction he has made for our sin, turning all our blame into everlasting honour. Where also our Lord says: 'Behold and see! For by the same might, wisdom and goodness I shall make well all that is not well; and you shall see it.' And because of this, he wants us to keep ourselves in the faith and truth of holy Church, not wanting to know his secrets now, except those that belong to us in this life.

The FOURTEENTH is that our Lord is the ground of our beseeking*[2]. And in this were seen two properties: one is rightful prayer, the other sure trust — both these he wants us to have in full measure. This way our prayer pleases him, and he will bring it to fruition by his goodness.

The FIFTEENTH is that we will suddenly be taken from all our pain and all our woe; and by his goodness we shall come up above, where we shall have our Lord Jesus as our reward and be filled full of joy and bliss in heaven.

The SIXTEENTH is that the blissful* Trinity our Maker, in

---

[2] Julian will have more to say about prayer in chs. 10, 41 etc. Her word *beseekeing* carries more the meaning of seeking (in faith) than asking or beseeching. And she will define it (ch. 41) as 'a new and gracious lasting will of the soul by which it is oned and fastened into the will of our Lord by the sweet, privy work of the Holy Spirit.'

Christ Jesus our Saviour, dwells unceasingly in our soul, worshipfully ruling and governing all things, mightily and wisely saving us and keeping us by and in his love. And we shall not be overcome by our enemy.

2

Julian begins to tell her story; how she prayed to God to intervene in her life by granting her three gifts, upon certain conditions.

THESE Revelations were shown to a simple creature that could not letter in the year of our Lord 1373, on the eighth day of May. Which creature had first desired three gifts from God. The first was a mind of his passion; the second was a bodily sickness in her youth at thirty years of age; and the third was to have of God three wounds.

As for the first, although I believed I already had some feeling for Christ's passion, yet I desired more by the grace of God. I thought at that time to be like Mary Magdalen and others who were Christ's lovers, and therefore I desired a bodily sight wherein I might have more knowledge of the bodily pains of our Saviour, and of the compassion of our Lady and all his true lovers that saw his pains in that time; for I would be one of them and suffer with him. I desired no other sight or showing of God until the time came for me to die. The cause of this petition was that after the showing I should have a more true mind of the passion of Christ.

The second request came to mind with contrition, freely desiring that it be a grave sickness, even to the point of death (so long as I might receive all the last rites of the Church); I imagined that I would feel myself nearly dying and that those around me would believe the same. For I would have no manner of comfort as to this earthly life. But in this sickness I desired to have all manner of pains both in body and spirit that I should have if I should die, with all the dreads and tempests of the fiends, except the outpassing of the soul.

I meant in this way to be purged by the mercy of God because of that sickness; and that would also speed* me in my death, for I desired soon to be with my God.

These two desires, for the passion and the sickness, I desired with a condition, saying thus: 'Lord, you know well what it is I want, if it be your will that I have it; or if it be not your will, good Lord, be not displeased, for I will nothing save as you will.'

As to the third gift, by the grace of God and teaching of holy Church, I conceived a mighty desire to receive three wounds in my life: that is to say the wound of true contrition, the wound of kind* compassion and the wound of wilful longing to God. And all this last petition I asked for without condition. The first two desires passed from my mind, but the third dwelled with me continually.

3

WHEN I was thirty and a half years old, God sent me a bodily sickness in which I lay for three days and three nights; and on the fourth night I took all my rites of holy Church and did not believe to live till day. And after this I languished for two days and two nights. And on the third night I oftentimes thought to have passed and so thought they that were with me. And being still young, I thought it a great sadness to die. It was not that I was attached to anything on this earth or that I feared bodily pain, for I put my trust in God and his mercy. Rather I wanted to live so that I might come to love God the better and for a longer while; then, grown to this greater love by means of his grace, I would come to know and love God more in the joys of heaven. For I was sure time spent in this present life would seem as nothing compared to the endless bliss that was to come. So I began to think: 'Good Lord, perhaps my living is not to your worship* any longer?' And I understood in my reason and by the pains I felt that I should die. And I assented fully to all, with all the will of my heart, to be at God's will.

I endured till day and by then I felt my body was dead from the middle downwards. Then I was lifted into a sitting position and propped up so as to have more freedom of heart to wait on God's will, thinking only of God while my life would last. My curate was called for to be at my ending, and by the time he came I had set my eyes and might no longer speak. He set the cross before my face and said: 'I have brought you the image of your Maker and Saviour: look upon him and find your comfort there.' I thought to myself that I was well, for my eyes were set upwards towards heaven where I trusted to come by the mercy of God. But nevertheless, I assented to set my eyes upon the face of the crucifix if I might, and so I did, for it seemed to me that I might manage to look longer straight ahead than upwards. After this my sight began to fail and it was all dark about me in the chamber as if it had been night, save in the image of the cross wherein I beheld a common light, and I knew not how. All beside the cross was ugly to me as if it had been much occupied by fiends.

Next my upper body began to die; I scarcely had any feeling and I was short of breath. Now I felt truly I would die. Yet of a sudden, all my pain was taken away from me, and I was healthy again as before, at least in my upper body. I marvelled at this sudden change for I thought to myself it was a secret working of God rather than any natural cause. Yet feeling this greater ease was never reason to trust that I would be more likely to live; nor was this ease complete, for I still thought I would prefer to be delivered from this world.

Then it suddenly came to me to ask for the second wound: that, by our Lord's gift and his own grace, I might truly feel his blissful passion. I simply wanted his pains to be my pains, such was my feeling for him; for now I could only long for God. But all the while I never looked for any vision or revelation: I simply wanted the same compassion that any good soul would have with our Lord Jesus who for love of us had willingly taken on our mortal flesh; and therefore I desired to suffer with him.

THE FIRST SHOWING

4

Julian's intuition that Christ's passion stands at the centre of our encounter with God is confirmed as she receives the first showing. The intimacy she describes is at first overpowering: here we have our first taste of Julian's self-effacing role as messenger.

Now at once I saw red blood trickling down from under the garland. Hot and freely it fell, copious and real it was, as if it had just been pressed down upon his blessed head, who is truly both God and man, the very same that suffered thus for me. In that moment, I knew clearly that it was he himself who showed me, without intermediary of any kind.

Within this same showing, suddenly the Trinity filled my whole heart full of utmost joy. I knew then that heaven will be like this for all who come to it, without end:

> For the Trinity is God,
> and God is the Trinity.
> The Trinity is our Maker and Keeper,*
> The Trinity is our everlasting Lover,
> everlasting joy and bliss, by our Lord Jesus Christ.

This was shown to me in the first and in all other showings:

that where Jesus appears, the Blessed Trinity is understood. That is how I saw this showing.

And I exclaimed: 'Benedicite, Domine!'

I meant this greeting reverently, yet it came as a great shout. For I wanted to thank our Lord, who is so reverent, so holy and apart, for being so homely* with a sinful creature who was still alive in this wretched flesh. I realized then that our Lord Jesus, with his courteous* love, wanted to comfort me ahead of my temptation that was to come; for it would come as no surprise if God permitted me, albeit in the safety of his grace, to be tempted by fiends before I died. Yet in this sight of his blessed passion and the Godhead that I saw with my full understanding, I knew well that it was strength enough for me (and for that matter all who are to be saved) to withstand all the fiends of hell and any other ghostly temptation.

Next he brought our blessed Lady to my understanding. I saw her with my understanding as though she were with me physically:[3] a simple maid and meek, so young she seemed like a mere child – yet the very same age when she conceived. And God showed me then something of the wisdom and truth of her soul. In particular, I saw her attitude towards God her Maker, how she marvelled with great reverence when he wished to be born of her, who was a mere and simple creature he himself had made. It was this wisdom, this truth, seeing how great was her Maker compared to her own littleness, that made her say to Gabriel, 'Behold me, God's handmaid.'

Then I knew for certain that she was more worthy and more full of grace than all the rest of God's creation, with the sole exception of the manhood of Christ.[4]

---

[3] I saw her ghostly in bodily likeness ...

[4] Julian means all that she declares of our Lady's pre-eminence among the human race: yet she recognizes that Mary's response to God is inaugural, so that our Fiat too must be uniquely our own and indeed no less total than hers.

5

*The intimacy of God's continual presence is like our clothing. The sight of
a hazelnut presents an image of the futility of created things which,
nonetheless, can block us from God.*

WHILE I still had sight of our Lord's head as it bled, he
showed me further understanding of his homely love. I
saw that he is the ground of all that is good and sup-
porting for us. He is our clothing that lovingly wraps and folds us
about; it embraces us and closes us all around as it hangs upon us
with such tender love; for truly he can never leave us. This made
me see that he is for us everything that is good.

At the same time, he showed me something small, about the
size of a hazelnut, that seemed to lie in the palm of my hand
as round as a tiny ball. I tried to understand the sight of it, won-
dering what it could possibly mean. The answer came: 'This is all
that is made.' I felt it was so small that it could easily fade to nothing; but again I was told: 'This lasts and it will go on lasting forever because God loves it. And so it is with every being that God
loves.'

I saw three properties about this tiny object. First, God had
made it: second, God loves it; and third, that God keeps it. Yet
what this really means to me, that he is the Maker, the Keeper,
the Lover, I cannot begin to tell. For until I am fully one with
him, I can never have full rest nor true bliss;[5] that is to say, until
I am so at one with him that no thing created comes between us,
my God and me. We must come to realize this: created things are
nothing, and we must turn aside from them to love and have our
God who is not made. This is the only reason why we are not
fully at ease in heart and soul: that we look to find our true rest

---

[5] *bliss*: the true and perfect happiness of heaven (cf. ch. 3). One of Julian's
keywords which is (among others) retained throughout the text and listed in
the glossary. Sometimes used in surprising yet deliberate conjunction, e.g. his
blissid passion means his 'sufferings by which we come to bliss' (ch. 8).

in these things that are so little that they contain no rest. And we know not our God, who is almighty, all wise, all good. For he is the very* rest. God will be known;[6] he is pleased when we find our rest in him. All that falls short of him will never satisfy us. This is why no soul can be at peace until it is rid[7] of all created things. Only when the soul turns away and denies itself so as to find him who is All will it be able to receive true peace and rest.

And I saw quite clearly how much God is pleased when a person comes to him in all simplicity, as it were quite naked, unafraid and trusting. This is the kind[8] yearnings of the soul as it is touched by the Holy Spirit, according to the understanding I have of this showing:

'God, of your goodness, give me yourself;
for you are enough to me;
and I may nothing ask that is less that may be full worship
 to you.
And if I ask anything that is less,
I am ever left wanting;
but only in you I have all.'

These words are are full lovesome to the soul and closely touch the will of God and his goodness. For his goodness fills all his creatures and spills into all that he does. He is our endless home: he only made us for himself; he remakes us by his blessed passion and always keeps us in his blessed love. All this is down to his goodness.

---

[6] Julian enjoys using compacted words that lead in two or more directions at once. The mystical writer Maggie Ross calls them 'wordknots'. Thus, *God will* means 'he will' (future) and 'he desires and decrees'.

[7] *nowted*: 'emptied' or 'rid'.

[8] Julian uses this key word throughout to represent the failed core, the old Adam, in us. And she distinguishes it from our substance. As man, she tells us, Christ took both our kind and our substance. Our substance remains pure and unsullied with him: *kind* is the subject of his 'again-making' or redemption, the 'working' of his mercy and grace with which we are intimately involved.

6

I understood this revelation to teach our soul to cling fast to the goodness of God. At the same time, I remembered all the different ways we are accustomed to pray and how busy we become when we lose sight of how God loves us. For I was persuaded at this time that what pleases God, what delights him most, is when we pray simply trusting in his goodness, holding on to him, relying upon his grace, with true understandingand steadfast by love, rather than if we made all the means that heart can think. Even when we summon all such skills, we are bound to fall short: all we need do is trust in God's own goodness for this will never fail us.

There came to mind then how numerous were all these different ways of prayer: how we are wont to pray to God by his holy Flesh, by his precious Blood, or his holy Passion – his most dear Death, his honourable Wounds. But the blessings, and eternal life that stems from this, all come from the same goodness of God. It is the same when we pray to him for love of his sweet Mother who bore him: this too is from God's goodness. Or we might pray by the holy Cross on which he died; but all the power and help that derives from that cross, this again is due to his goodness. And so it is also with all the special help we have from the saints and all the company of heaven, that is to say the very dear love and the never-ending friendship we have with them: it is of his goodness. The means afforded by the goodness of God are so plentiful in number; but chief among them is the blessed kind that he took to himself of the Maiden, together with all the means that belong to our redemption and our endless salvation both before and after.

It follows that he is well pleased when we seek and pray to him by these means; yet we should realize and know that he is the goodness that underlies them all.[9]

---

9 Hearing Julian's almost frantic plea for simplicity in our praying, we can recall the clutter of religious practice of her day and feel complacent. Yet we too can bring similar clutter that crowds God out when we pray.

For the goodness of God is the highest prayer and it comes down to us to meet our very least need. It quickens our soul and brings it to life; it makes it grow in grace and virtue; moreover it is nearest in kind and readiest in grace; the very same grace the soul hungers after now and always, until we know him verily that has us all in himself beclosed.

So it is that a man walks erect; he eats the food for his body that is then hidden away within as it were in a fine purse. And when it is the time of his necessity, the purse is opened and shut again – modestly and without show. And that all this is God's doing is shown by his words when he tells us that[10] he comes down to the lowest part of our need. For he never despises that which he himself has made. Neither is he reluctant to serve our simplest office that belongs to our body in kind, because he loves our soul that he made in his own likeness.

For just as the body is clad in clothes and the flesh in skin and the bones in flesh with the heart in the breast, so are we, soul and body, clothed and wrapped around in the goodness of God. Yet it is even more homely than this; because they all disappear once they decay. But the goodness of God is always whole and more near to us without any comparison. It is true that our Lover desires the soul to stay close to him with all its strength, clinging ever more tightly to his goodness. Of all things the heart may think, this pleases God the most and affords us much progress. Our soul is loved so preciously by him, our highest good, that it is beyond all human understanding. In truth, no human alive can fathom how much, how sweetly and tenderly, our Maker loves us. And so we are able by the help of his grace to stay beholding in prayer this lofty, surpassing and immeasurable love that almighty God has towards us of his goodness.

---

[10] 'So it is ... tells us that': this remarkable passage, earthy yet discreet, does not appear in Sloane 2499 but only in the Paris MS. It is included accepting that Julian herself wrote it, rather than it being some later addition. Its very boldness would seem to indicate this conclusion. Moreover it bridges the sense from the previous paragraph in typical manner with authentic voice.

And this means that we may ask our Lover with reverence anything we wish; for our dearest kindly will is to have God, and his good will is to have us. Nor can we cease in our desire to love and have him until it is fulfilled in endless joy. Then we will want no more. For now it is his will that we be busy knowing and loving him until that time comes to fulfilment in heaven; which was the meaning and purpose of this teaching of love that was shown, as you will see presently. The strength and the ground of everything was to be shown in the first revelation. For of all thing, the beholding and the loving of the Maker makes the soul seem least in its own sight and most fills it with reverent dread and true meekness with plenty of charity to all its fellow Christians.

7

WISHING to teach us this important lesson, as it seemed to me, our Lord God showed me our Lady St Mary, as she was at that time; that is to say the high wisdom and truth she had as she beheld* her Maker, he being so great. This greatness and the nobility of her contemplating God filled her full of holy dread*; and by comparison she saw herself so little and so low, so simple and so poor in regard to her Lord God, that this reverend dread also filled her with meekness. This then was the ground by which she was filled all full of grace with every kind of virtue overpassing* all creatures.

And all the while he showed me this (as I said before, in a spiritual way), I could see a bodily vision of his head bleeding freely. Great drops of blood fell from under the garland; like pellets they seemed to come straight from the veins. As they appeared they were a reddish brown, for the bleeding was copious; but when they began to spread, they seemed to turn a bright red. As they reached the eyebrows, suddenly they vanished.

And all the while this bleeding was still visible, I came to see and understand many things. Yet there was nothing like its vivid, lifelike quality. For the sheer flow of blood was like drops of water coming from thatch eaves after a heavy shower of rain, when they come so thick and fast that you may not chance to count them. Again, as they spread all rounded across the forehead, I was reminded of herring scales. In fact, I could not rid my mind of these three homely images – pellets, so round were the droplets as they first appeared; herring scales for their same roundness as they spread; rain-drops from the eaves of a house, so countless were they in number.

This showing was vivid and lifelike, hideous and dreadful, sweet*[11] and lovely. But of all the things I saw, this was my greatest comfort: that our good Lord, who is so holy and so much to be feared is at the same instant so homely and courteous. This warmed me full of love and comforted my very soul.

To make this quite clear to me, he showed me a simple example. The most honour that a solemn king or a great lord can offer a poor servant, is to show his feelings both privately and in public as they truly are – with smiles and approval. Then will this poor creature think thus: 'Ah, what might this noble Lord do for me that gives more honour and joy than to show me that am so simple such marvellous homeliness?'

This bodily example was enough to overpower any man's heart and carry him out of himself for pure joy at such great homeliness. For this is the manner in which our Lord Jesus would deal with us. For it seems to me our greatest possible joy that he who is highest and mightiest, most noble and worthy, is at once so lowly, meek and most homely and most courteous. In truth and deed will this marvellous joy be fully ours when we shall see him. Thus it is our Lord's will that we want

---

[11] The word 'sweet' has today become utterly debased both as to taste and as to emotion: Julian uses it in its simple and original sense: 'pertaining to a sensual, pure taste', that elevates the soul to higher contemplation and in particular to an awareness of the presence and activity of Christ.

13

and trust him, rejoice and savour him, take comfort and good heart as far as possible until the time comes when at last we know all this for good. For the perfection of our joy, as I believe, is this marvellous courtesy and homeliness from our Father, who is our Maker, in our Lord Jesus Christ, who is both our Brother and our Saviour.

But on this earth no one can know this marvellous homeliness, unless our Lord shows it specially, or with some excess of grace it is given inwardly of the Holy Spirit. But faith and belief, together with charity, deserves such a reward; and so it is to be had by grace. For our whole life is grounded in faith, along with hope and charity. And the showing, given to whomsoever it pleases God to give it, plainly demonstrates this fact, albeit openly, by revealing all manner of secrets pertaining to our faith and belief which it helps to understand. But when the showing, which can only be a passing experience, fades, it is kept by faith and the grace of the Holy Spirit until our dying day.

So that this revelation is none other than the faith we all hold, no more no less, and this is our Lord's meaning when he allows it to come to an end.

8

ALL the while I saw this copious bleeding, I could not cease from saying 'Benedicite Domine!' In this revelation I understood six points: the first is the signs of his blessed[12] passion and the plentiful shedding of his precious blood; the second is the Maiden that is his own dear Mother;

---

[12] blissid: 'blessed' in the sense of bringing bliss. Yet the first blessing (Exodus 12.13) was in blood; thus Julian identifies Christ's passion as the source of future bliss.

the third is the blissful* Godhead that always was, is and ever shall be, all mighty, all wise and all love; the fourth is all that he has made – I know full well both heaven and earth and all things he has made are great and large, fair and good: only it seemed so little in my sight because it was shown in the presence of him who is the Maker of it all. When a soul sees the Maker, all that he made appears as a very little thing. The fifth is the Maker of all that made it for love: and by this same love is it kept,[13] and shall be without end, as I have said earlier; the sixth is that God is all that is good, and the good that is in all things, that is he, as I see it.

Our Lord showed me all this in the first showing, giving me the space and time to contemplate it all. Then, once the bodily sight faded, I was left with a spiritual vision in my understanding. I stayed with this in holy fear, glad at what I saw, yet bold enough to want to see more if he would show me, or to stay for longer with what was before me. All the while I felt great love towards all my fellow Christians; for I wanted them all to share my understanding of everything I saw – I knew it would comfort them. And I felt sure that this revelation was for all the world to see.

Then I said to those at my bedside: 'Today is my last when I will be judged.' I told them so because I thought I was sure to die; for when a man or woman comes to die, then their judgement lasts for all time, as I understand it. This was why I spoke these words to them: I wanted them to love God more, to remember how short life is and to learn a lesson from me. All the while, although I was certain that I would die, which was both a wonder to me as well as partial sadness, yet I was sure that this vision was also shown for the living.

Everything I say about myself, that also goes for all my

---

[13] Julian's notion of keeping is again a key concept. The Maker is both our creator and initiator yet – like a gardener who sows in order to tend – he too keeps and nurtures us. This she describes as God's working, with which she would have us collaborate continually.

fellow Christians. For this is what I understood from our Lord, that this is his meaning. And so I beg you all, for God's sake, and I advise you for your own advantage, to ignore this wretch that it was shown to in the first place, and attend instead with all your might and wit and meekness to God. For it was by his courteous love and from his endless goodness that he wanted to show it to everyone, for the comfort of us all. Thus God truly wants you to receive it with every joy and gladness just as if Jesus himself had shown it to you all in person.

9

I myself am not a good person merely because I received these showings; they will only make me a better Christian if I come to love God more. And inasmuch as you come to a greater love of God through them, then will you profit more than I. Here I am not talking to the wise, who already know as much, but to simple folk, for your help and comfort. For in truth, I was never shown that God loved me more than the least soul that stands in his grace; indeed I am certain there be many who have had neither sight nor showing save that of the common teaching of holy Church, yet they love God better than I. For when I look to myself as a single individual, then I am nothing. But all my hope comes from being united in one love with all my fellow Christians. For on this unity the life of all that shall be saved depends.

God is all that is good, as to my sight. God has made all things that are made; and God loves all that he has made. So that he who loves all his fellow Christians in general, seeing how God has made them, loves everything it is possible to love. For in humankind that is to be saved is gathered in everything made, yes and God that is unmade too: for in humankind there is God: and in God is all. So that he that loves like this, loves all. I am sure by God's grace that he who attends to this will be taught aright and will find true comfort each according to his need.

I speak only of those that shall be saved, for this is all God showed me at this time. But I only hold as true those things of faith that holy Church preaches and teaches. For I hold to the faith of the Church that I knew before this revelation, in which faith I hope, by God's grace, I will always stand firm in both practice and custom; and I never desired to receive them in any contrary manner. This was my intention and my only aim as I attended as carefully as possible to the showing; for in all this blessed showing I attended to God's meaning alone.

The revelation as a whole was given in three ways:[14] by bodily vision, by words given directly to my understanding and by spiritual enlightenment. Of this latter spiritual vision, I cannot speak clearly nor may I as fully as I might wish. Yet I trust our Lord God of his loving goodness will make you receive its inner message more sweetly than I can or might ever tell it.

---

[14] Here Julian is describing the three ways in which she perceived her visions. They conform to the classic and received understanding of God communicating mystically with us, as has been discussed in the preface.

10

Julian speaks of our common working in this life; how
we are to fall into step with all that Christ has achieved in his
passion, the chief being that we are able to 'seek him continually'.
This seeking is the working of the Holy Spirit that leads us
towards our coming bliss. And we must 'seek with a will gladly
and merrily'; and all the while, though 'for his working is
secret ... yet he will be perceived'.

AFTER this, I saw with bodily sight the face of the crucifix that hung before me, which I beheld[15] continually, a part of his passion: contempt, spitting, soiling and buffeting as well as many distressing pains – more than I can tell – and frequent changing of colour. At one time, I saw how half the face, beginning from the ear, was completely covered with dried blood yet ending in mid-face; and after that, the other half, in the same way; and this part vanished continually as soon as it came. I saw this bodily, yet it was dark and mournful so that I wanted more light in order to see it more clearly. And I was answered in my reason: 'If God will show you more, he shall be your light.'[16] For I saw him yet I sought him.

For we are so blind here, so unwise, that we never seek God until in his goodness he shows himself to us. And if we glimpse him through grace, then are we stirred by the same grace to seek him with great desire so as to see him more blissfully.

---

[15] *beheld*: Julian uses 'behold' as a threshold word which merely opens a door to unmeaning, a mystery that is beyond words. Beholding is not so much rumination but contemplation, the still enjoyment of an exchange between God and the soul that is beyond human words or expression.

[16] Typical example of Julian's wordknots: the pun on 'will' suspends the promise, throwing it back into God's time and good will, i.e., 'God will show you when he will(s).' And this runs on into the next phrase, 'he shall be your light'.

And thus I saw him and I sought him; I had him, yet I wanted him. And this is and should be our common working* in this life, as I see it.

There was one time when my understanding was led down into the seabed, and there I saw hills and dales, all green as if the seaweed and gravel were overgrown with moss. Then I understood that if any man or woman were under the deep sea and have sight of God, knowing God as he truly is, with us continually, then they would be safe in body and soul: indeed, they would have more solace and comfort than the whole world could tell. For he wants us to believe that we see him continually, even though it seems to us that we see him very little, since in this way he will make us daily grow in grace. For he will be seen and he will be sought; he will be waited for and he will be trusted.

This second showing was so low and so little and so simple that my spirits were in great trouble at the beholding,[17] mournful with fear and longing; so that sometimes I doubted that it was a showing at all. And then at other times, our good Lord gave me better sight so that I understood that it was indeed a showing – a figure or likeness of our foul mortal skin[18] that our fair, bright, blessed Lord bore for our sins. It made me think of the holy vernicle in Rome[19] on which he left the imprint of his own blessed face which, at the time of his hard passion, would have often changed colour as he went willingly to his death; and given its browning and blackening, so piteous and drawn, many wondered how it could be so, since he portrayed it there

[17] Again, Julian means that this exchange between God and herself must be worked at and sustained – and in this instance with great difficulty.

[18] *dede-hame*: *dede* means 'dead' or 'mortal' and *hame* means both 'home' and an ox's yoke – hence the fleshly home in which Christ dwelt plus the yoke 'he bore for our sins'.

[19] The Holy Veil with which Veronica was said to have wiped Jesus' face as he made his way to Calvary. Julian would have heard pilgrims' firsthand accounts of seeing this holy relic; we know she was visited by Margery Kempe who pilgrimaged widely to Jerusalem, to Aachen, Assisi and Rome as well as Santiago de Compostella.

with his very own blessed face which is the fairest in heaven, flower of the earth, fruit of the Maiden's womb. How then could this image be so discoloured and so far from fair? Now I wish to tell of the understanding I have come to by God's grace.

We know in our faith and through our belief in the teaching and preaching of the holy Church that the blessed Trinity made humanity to his image and in his likeness. In the same manner we know that humankind fell by sin so wretchedly and so deeply that there was no other way to restore us than by him who made us. He who made humankind by love, in the same love would restore us to the same bliss, even overpassing[20] it. For just as we were made like to the Trinity in our first making, our maker wants us to be like Jesus Christ our Saviour, in heaven without end, by virtue* of our again-making.[21] Now between these two happenings, for love and honour of humankind, he would make himself like us in this mortal life, in all our foulness and wretchedness, so that we may be without guilt. As has already been said this means it was in the image and likeness of our own foul dead skin that our fair, bright, blessed Lord lies hidden. But I am sure it is true to say – and we should trust as much – that there was none fairer man until such time as his fine colour was changed by the travail and sorrow and passion of dying. More is said of this in the eighth revelation, which also deals with this likeness; so too of the vernicle of Rome, whose diverse changes of colour and expression, now comforting and enlivening, at other times more wretched and deadly, can also be seen there.

---

[20] Wordknot: overpass/passover. ME *overpass* is the equivalent to our 'surpass'; yet the knot remains to remind us that Christ, in his remaking of us, is our Paschal benefactor, bringing us yet more benefits than were ever given to Adam and Eve.

[21] *be the vertue of our geynmakyng*: this key phrase announces Julian's understanding of the central mystery of our again-making (rather than 'redemption', our 'being bought back'). The virtue is Christ's alone: dying as man he empowers us with his love, making us a second time – overpassing, as Julian puts it, his first creation, Adam.

By this sight I was taught to understand that our soul's continual seeking pleases God greatly; for we can do no more than seek, suffer and trust, and it is worked in the soul by the Holy Spirit; and when we find him clearly this is by special grace at a time he chooses. Seeking with faith, hope and charity pleases our Lord; and finding pleases the soul and fills it full of joy. And so I was taught to understand that seeking is as good as beholding, all the while he allows the soul to labour. It is God's will that we continue to seek him and strive to behold him, waiting for the moment when he chooses by special grace to show us himself. This does him the most honour and profits you; it happens gently and effectively with the guiding grace of the Holy Spirit. For when a soul fastens itself to God truly trusting, whether in seeking or beholding, this is the best service it may render him, as I see it.[22]

These are the two workings to be seen in this vision: one is the seeking, the other beholding. The seeking is common; for this every soul may have with God's grace, and ought to have and achieve with discernment and the teaching of the holy Church. It is God's will that we have three things in our seeking. The first is that we seek with a will gladly and merrily, busily and without sloth, as much as his grace allows, avoiding both the shackles of heaviness and the luxury of sorrow. The second is that we abide steadfastly in his love, without grousing and striving against him, until our life's end, for this lasts but a while. The third, that we mightily trust in him, full of faith, for it is his will.

We know he will appear suddenly and blissfully to all his lovers; for his working is secret, yet he will be perceived, and his appearing will be swift and sudden; and he will be trusted, for he is full gracious and homely – blessed may he be!

---

[22] The very manner in which Julian herself appears to labour over this extended passage imitates the sweat and toil we daily experience in our prayer. She is never tempted to tell us: hang in for the breakthrough. Rather, her reasons for sustaining the effort are selfless: that God is pleased thereby, that the Holy Spirit is with us all the while, that in his own good time he will give us 'beholding'.

11

Julian begins to expound the message that stands central to her showings:
God is active throughout the entire working of the universe —
'see I do all thing'. In himself, he is rightful: he has
no need of grace and mercy. Thus she saw 'God in a point'.
But he is also the mid-point as he acts outside himself, guiding all things
to the end his wisdom has set. So that there appears to be no room for sin;
this mystery she leaves for later. We start with the positive vision of a
hands-on God who is governing all to his preordained liking.

AFTER this I saw God in a point,[23] that is to say, in my understanding, and in this sight I saw that he is in all things. I beheld attentively, seeing and knowing in the sight. And as I marvelled quietly, a soft dread came over me so that I asked in my mind: 'What is sin?' For I saw clearly that God does all things, even the very least. I knew truly that nothing happens by chance or accident, but all is by the foreseeing wisdom of God. Even if it seems by chance or accident in our sight, that is due to blindness or shortsightedness on our part. For these things are in God's foreseeing wisdom from without beginning (indeed he leads them all rightfully, gloriously, continually to their best end); yet as they come about, they fall upon us suddenly to take us unawares. And thus, by our blindness and lack of foresight, we see them as mishaps or accidents; but it is not like that with God. Therefore I needs must recognize that all that is done, it is well done, for our Lord does all. But at this time, creatures' deeds were not shown, but only our Lord working in the creature. For he is in the mid-point of all things and he does all things; yet I was sure he did not sin. And

---

[23] This striking metaphor is multi-headed: God is the still centre of creation; he is without dimension, immeasurable; he is without time — the point outside time that is discontinuous because eternal.

here I saw truly that sin is no-deed, for in all this sin was never shown. I could no longer marvel at this but beheld our Lord and whatever he would show me.

For a while, therefore, the rightful* workings of God were shown to this soul. Rightfulness has two fair properties: it is right and it is full.24 And even so are all the works of God our Lord; and to them belongs neither the work of mercy nor grace, for where nothing fails, all is right. (Later, at another time, I shall tell how he showed me the vision of sin nakedly, when he uses the work of mercy and grace.)

Now this vision was shown to my understanding, for our Lord wants the soul truly turned so as to behold him and all his works in general. For they are full of goodness, all his doings are easy and sweet; and at once the soul is eased when it turns from our own blind judgement towards the fair, sweet judgement of God.

While to us some deeds may seem well done, others evil, this is not so in God's sight. For since all things have their ground in God's making, so all that is done belongs to God's doing. It is easy to understand that the best things are well done: yet as equally well as the best and highest deed is done, so too is the least thing well done; and all because it belongs to the order God ordained from without beginning, for he is the only doer. I saw full surely that he never changes his purpose in any manner of thing, nor will he without end. For there was nothing that he did not know that he has not rightfully ordained without any beginning; therefore all was set in order, including all things made, as they would stand without end. Thus no single thing shall fail at the point that he made them all fully good; therefore the blessed Trinity is always fully pleased in all his works. And all this he showed most blissfully, and this was his meaning:

---

24 Julian alights upon this apparent tautology with customary skill: at first its meaning defeats us, but by lingering with this wordknot, her purposeful truth becomes vividly apparent.

See I am God.

See I am in all thing.

See I do all thing.

See I never lift my hands off my own works, nor ever shall, without end.

See I lead all thing to the end I ordained for it from without beginning with the same might, wisdom and love that I made it.

How should anything be amiss?

Thus mightily, wisely and lovingly was the soul examined in this vision. Then I saw truly that I needs must assent with great reverence, simply enjoying in God.

THE FOURTH SHOWING

12

Julian sees the passion and Christ's death both literally and in image,
the act when he spills his blood copiously, to the last drop. His act
bursts the bonds of hell, releasing all those waiting in that dark place —
from Adam onwards; his act upon the cross stands too as a pledge
'to wash all creatures ... still to come'.

AFTER this I saw in my beholding that the body seemed to be bleeding plenteously due to the scourging. And this is how it looked: the fair skin was deeply broken into the tender flesh with the sharp beating all across the sweet body; so plenteously did the hot blood run out that there was neither skin nor even wound, but it seemed as if it were all blood. And when it came to the point where it should have spilled down, then it vanished; notwithstanding, the bleeding continued for a while when it could be seen by looking closely. And this seemed so plenteous to me, that I thought if it had been real and actually happening then, it would have soaked the bed in blood and spilled over all around.[25] Then I was reminded how God had made the waters of the earth so plentiful in our service to meet our bodily comfort, all for tender love that he has for us; yet he likes it better that we take his blessed blood quite naturally to wash away sin. There is no liquid made that he prefers to give us; for it is most plenteous as it is most precious, by virtue of the blessed Godhead. It is our birthright[26] and blissfully flows to us by virtue of his precious love. The dear and worthy blood of our Lord Jesus Christ, as truly as it is most precious, so truly is it plentiful. Behold and see: this precious and plenteous, worthy and dear blood descended down into hell, burst forth her bonds and delivered all there who belonged to the court of heaven.[27] The precious plenty of his dear and worthy blood overflows the whole earth and is ready to wash from sin all creatures of good will, both those that have been and those still to come. This same precious plenty of his dearworthy blood goes up into heaven in the blessed body of our Lord Jesus Christ; it is there within him bleeding and praying for us to the Father; and this is and shall be for as long as it is needed. And evermore it flows throughout heaven enjoying the salvation of all humankind that are and shall be there, fulfilling the number that fails.

---

[25] Such gruesome realism would not have seemed the same in Julian's day. In place of bloody depictions of the crucifixion, perhaps we should be content to substitute the violence of the cinema screen or the realism of television world news. Her meaning remains, at very least, a vivid metaphor of Christ's intervention within human history.

[26] *it is our kinde*: it belongs to us by nature.

[27] The 'harrowing of hell': not the place of eternal doom but a waiting place to which Christ descended after his death so as to release its many prisoners including all the saints of the Old Covenant from Adam onwards – a popular theme of her day which Julian would have seen represented in church murals. Note she sees 'hell' as feminine ('her bonds'), as if it were a womb containing all who are now to be delivered by Christ to his Father.

13

How the fiend is overcome by our Lord's blessed passion. And how
a property of God is his unchanging purpose.

AFTER this, without any words, God allowed me to behold
him for a considerable time, taking in all that I had
seen, understanding all that was contained therein, as
much as my simple soul might. And then without voice or any
opening of lips, there formed in my soul these words: 'Here is
how the fiend is overcome.'

Our Lord spoke these words, meaning his blessed passion, as
he had already shown before. In this our Lord showed that his
blessed passion is the overcoming of the fiend. God showed that
the fiend has the same malice now as before the Incarnation;
and yet although he labours as hard now, he continually sees
all those saved souls escape him, wonderfully by virtue of
Christ's precious passion. This is a sorrow to him, an evil reality of which he is ashamed; for all that God allows him to do
turns to our joy, yet to him it is constant shame and woe. This
means that he has as much sorrow when God permits him to
work as when he is prevented; and he can never do so much
evil as he wishes, for God has taken his power up into his own
hands. For as I see it, there can be no wrath with God, for he
is our endless Lord, having regard to his own honour as well
as the profit of all who will be saved. He withstands these
reproved beings with his might and right, while they in their
malice and waywardness are busy contriving how they might
go against God's will.

Also I saw how our Lord scorns his malice and deadens his
might, and he wills us to do the same. And at this sight I
laughed so mightily that I made those standing round laugh
with me. I thought how much I wanted all my fellow Christians

to have seen what I saw, for then could we all have laughed together. And although I did not see Christ laugh, yet I understood that we may rightly laugh, comforting ourselves and finding our joy in God because the devil is overcome. And when I saw him scorn his malice, it was a leading of my understanding into our Lord, that is to say an inward showing of truth without any change in his countenance. And this, as I see it, is a worshipful property* that is in God which is durable.

After this, I fell sad and said: 'I can see three things: game, scorn and earnest. The game I see is that the fiend is overcome; I see scorn that God scorns him and this will always be so; and I see earnest in that he is overcome by the blessed passion and death of our Lord Jesus Christ which was done in full earnest and with much sad labour.'

And I said: 'he is scorned', meaning that God scorns him; that is to say, because he sees him now just as shall be done to him without end – for God showed how the fiend is damned. That is to say, when I said 'he shall be scorned', this means generally he will be scorned at doomsday by all who shall be saved; while he will have great envy of their consolation. Then he shall see that all the woe and tribulation he has done them will be turned to increase their joy without end; and all the pain and tribulation that he would have brought upon them shall endlessly go with him into hell.

14

How we will be rewarded in heaven by three degrees of bliss,
God thanking us for our labour.

AFTER this our good Lord said: 'I thank you for your labour, namely that of your youth.' At this my understanding was lifted up to heaven where I saw our Lord as a Lord in his own house to which he has called all his most dear servants and friends to a solemn feast. I saw the Lord take no place of honour in his house, rather I saw him rule royally there filling it full of joy and mirth. He himself presided by endlessly gladdening and entertaining his very close friends with every warmth and courtesy, with a marvellous melody of endless love in his own fair blessed face. For it is to see the glorious Godhead in this way, face to face, that fills the very heavens with such joy and bliss.

God showed three degrees of bliss that belong to every soul in heaven who has served God in any way here on earth. The first is the thanks and due honour they will receive from our Lord God as soon as they are delivered from their pain; this thanks is so high and so heaped with honour that it seems as if it would quite fill them even were they to receive no more. For I thought to myself that all the sum of pain and labour suffered by all humanity might not deserve the honourable thanks that will be given to a single person who has willingly served God. The second is that all the blessed already in heaven will see this worshipful thanks as he makes his servant known to them all. And here an example was shown. For a king to thank his servants is a great honour, but when he also tells the whole realm, then this honour is so much greater. And the third is that, as new and pleasing as the thanks may be when first received, just so it shall continue to last without end. And I saw how homely and sweetly this was shown: that the life story of everyone shall be told in heaven and each shall be rewarded for the loyal service given through their days. And it will also be the same for those that willingly and freely offer their youth to God, they will be especially rewarded and wonderfully thanked; for I saw that whatever time and whenever man or woman truly turns to God, be it only for one day, they shall have all these three degrees of bliss.

And so the more a loving soul sees this courtesy of God, the more gladly will they serve him all the days of their life.

THE SEVENTH SHOWING

15

Julian is puzzled at her experience of alternations of weal and woe, especially when this does not appear to be directly connected to any sin on her part. She concludes that this is simply our human condition and the way our Lord keeps in touch with our feeling soul.

AFTER this he showed a sovereign spiritual loving in my soul. I was filled full of an everlasting sureness that took hold of me in power without any pain or dread. The feeling was so glad and so spiritual that I was in all peace and rest, so that nothing on earth might grieve me. Yet this lasted but a while; then I was changed, left to myself with all the heaviness and weariness of life – I was burdened with myself, so that I barely had patience to live. There was no comfort, no ease: only faith, hope and charity; and while I had these in reality, yet they were little in feeling. But soon enough our blessed Lord once again gave me that comfort and rest of soul, lovingly and surely, so blissful and so mighty that no dread nor sorrow nor pain that my body could have suffered would have diseased* me. And then I was shown once again that pain of feeling; then the loving joy: now the one,

29

and now the other, many times repeating – I suppose some twenty in all.

And in the times of joy, I might have said with St Paul: 'Nothing shall separate me from the love of Christ.' And when in pain, I might have cried out with Peter: 'Lord, save me for I perish.'

This vision was shown to my understanding, that it is necessary for some souls to feel this way, sometime in comfort and sometime failing, left all alone to themselves. For God wants us to know that it is he who keeps us surely whether we be in woe or weal. And for the good of our soul we are sometimes left to ourselves, without sin being always the cause; for at this time I had not sinned, for it was all so sudden, yet I was still left to myself. Equally, I did not deserve to have received all these feelings of bliss.

When it pleases him, our Lord gives freely of himself, and then sometimes he suffers us to feel in woe. Yet both are one and the same love; for it is God's will that we hold ourselves in his comfort with all our might. For bliss will last without end while pain passes and will be brought to nothing for those that will be saved. And therefore it is not God's will that we linger in feelings of pain by mourning and sorrowing over them, yet we should swiftly pass them by, keeping ourselves in his endless love.

16

Julian sees Christ's passion, beholding his face.
She describes a curious, hard wind that dried him as he died.

AFTER this Christ showed a part of his passion near his
death. I saw his sweet face as it was then, all dry and
bloodless with the pallor of dying. And by degrees it
grew still more pale, dead and listless; and then, as it became
almost lifeless, turning to blue. After this, as death itself
approached, the flesh turned from blue to brown. His passion
was shown me in his face, and in particular his lips; where
before they were fresh and ruddy and pleasing to my sight, I
now saw only these four colours. It was distressing to see the
change wrought in this deep dying; for instance I noticed the
nose was clogged and dried, and the sweet body was brown
and black, quite bled of his own fair, lively colour by this dry
dying. For at the time our Lord and blessed Saviour died upon
the cross, there was a dry, hard wind – and I saw it was wondrous cold. And when the precious blood was bled from the
sweet body, all that might pass out from it, yet there still
remained some moisture within the sweet flesh of Christ. It was
showed that the bloodshed and the pain of drying within and
the blowing of the wind and the cold from without came
together in the sweet body of Christ. And these four, the two
without and two within, dried the flesh of Christ as time
passed. And though this pain was bitter and sharp, it was equally long-lasting, as I saw it; and so all the lively spirit of Christ's
flesh was painfully dried up. And this is how I saw the sweet
flesh die; it seemed to happen part by part, all with most bitter pain. And as long as there was any spirit of life in Christ's
flesh, so long did he continue in pain. The length of his pain
seemed to me as if he had been near death for seven long

nights, all the while at the point of death and suffering his last pain. And when I say that it seemed to me that he had been seven days in his dying, I mean that the sweet body was so discoloured, so dried, so clogged, so deathly and so piteous as to seem he had been dead seven nights, yet dying all the while. And I thought in myself that this dying of Christ's flesh was the greatest and last pain of his passion.

17

The vivid almost intrusive realism of this passage will alarm and puzzle the contemporary reader. Yet it must be seen as a direct consequence of Julian's initial petition to experience the physical aspects of Christ's passion for herself. Moreover commentators have pointed out that her method here follows closely the school of affective prayer popular in her day; the classic example of this literal, almost photographic, approach to the sufferings of Christ is to be found in the popular medieval devotion of The Fifteen Oes of St Bridget of Sweden with its emphasis on visualizing the physical aspects of the passion in order to share its spiritual efficacy.[28]

THIS sight of his dying brought to my mind the words of Christ: 'I thirst'. For I saw in Christ a double thirst: one bodily, the other spiritual – which I will speak about in chapter 31.

As for his word, it was shown for the bodily thirst which I

---

[28] 'O Jesus, most profound abyss of mercy: I beseech you by the depth of your wounds, which pierced your flesh to the heart and very marrow of your bones, draw me from the depths of sin into which I have sunk, and hide me deep in the holes of your wounds from the face of your anger, Lord, until judgement is past.' – Eamon Duffy, *The Stripping of the Altars* (Yale University Press), pp. 248–56; see also Denise Nowakowski Baker, *Julian of Norwich's Showings* (Princeton University Press), pp. 44–7, for a detailed explanation of affective spirituality.

understood to be caused by lack of moisture, for the blessed flesh and bones were left all alone without blood and moisture. The blessed body dried for a long time and alone, with the piercing of the nails and the weight of the body. For I understood that with the size of the nails and their grievous hardness bearing into the tenderness of the sweet hands and the sweet feet, the wounds opened wider and the body sagged for all its weight during the long time it was hanging there; and what with this piercing and the wringing of the head with tightness of the crown, all became baked dry with blood: the sweet hair clung to it, the flesh clinging to the thorns as it dried and the thorns clinging to the drying flesh. To begin with, while the flesh was still fresh and bleeding, the continual pressure of the thorns made the wounds open wide. And then I began to see that the sweet skin and tender flesh, mixed with the hair and blood, was raised and had become loosened from the bone by the thorns, for they cut through and jagged it into many pieces. It sagged like a cloth and seemed about to fall off, for it was loose and had grown heavy with moisture. All this was a great sorrow and made me dread, for I thought I would not for my life have watched it fall. How this had been done, I could not see; but I understood that it was the sharp thorns and the rough and grievous way the garland had been set there, without sparing and without pity.

This continued for some time until soon it began to change; and still I beheld and marvelled how it could have been. Then I saw how it was, for as the flesh began to dry, so did it lose in part its weight as it became set about the garland. So it seemed now there were two circles, as if one garland had been laid upon another. The garland of thorns was now dyed with blood while the other garland as well as the head were all of the same brownish hue, the colour blood turns when it has dried. As for the skin upon the flesh, both in the face and on the body, it was now all wrinkled small and tannin colour, like a dry board when it is scorched, the face more than the body.

I saw four ways in which it had dried: the first that now it was bloodless, the second was the pain that followed after this, the third was hanging up in the air, just as people hang a cloth out to dry,[29] the fourth was that his human need was for liquid yet was no kind of comfort ministered to him in all his woe and disease. Ah! hard and grievous was his pain, but much more hard and grievous was the lack of moisture when everything began to congeal and dry. These were the pains shown me in the blissful head: the first caused by the dying while it was still moist; and the other, the slow, clinging drying from the wind blowing from without that dried him the more and pained him with cold so that it is more than my heart can think. These and all the other pains I saw, there is little that I can say, for it may never be told in full.

To see all these many pains of Christ filled me full of pain. I knew well enough that he suffered it only the once, but he wanted to show me his sufferings and to fill me with mind of it just as I had begged him at the outset.

And in all this time of Christ's pain I felt nothing other than for his pains. Until I thought to myself 'Little did I realise what pain it was I asked for', and like a wretch I regretted it, thinking to myself if only I had known what it were like, I would never have prayed for it. For I thought these pains of mine surpassed even those of bodily death, saying to myself, 'Is there any pain like this?' And the answer came into my head: 'Hell is another pain apart, for there is despair. But of all pains that lead to salvation, this pain is the most: to see your love suffer.' How might any pain be more to me than to see him who is my whole life, my bliss and all my joy suffer? Here I felt truly that I loved Christ so much above myself that there was no worse pain I might suffer than to see him in pain.

---

[29] In chapter 28, Julian uses the same metaphor when Christ speaks of the Church (in Paul's words, his own Body): 'God's servants ... holy Church, shall be shaken ... just as people shake a cloth in the wind.'

18

Julian's harsh and vivid realization of the passion is now transposed onto a spiritual plane. Contemplating our Lady's feelings as his mother, a fresh element of compassion is revealed that invites our own participation.

HERE I saw some part of the compassion of our Lady St Mary. For Christ and she were so united in love that the greatness of his loving was to cause her very great pain: in this I saw a substance* of kind love that creatures have towards him, continued by grace.[30] And this human love was generously, overpassingly shown in his sweet mother; for since she loved him more than all others, her pains exceeded theirs. For however much higher, mightier, sweeter the love is, the more sorrow it is to the lover to see the body they love in pain. All his disciples, all his true lovers suffered pains more than their own body's death; I am sure of this, from my own feelings, that the least of them loved him so far above themselves that it is more than I can say.

And in this I saw a great oneing between Christ and ourselves; I knew it to be so: for when he was in pain, we were in pain. And all creatures able to suffer, suffered pain with him — I am talking about all those creatures that God made to our service. The whole firmament, and the earth itself throughout its whole nature, failed for sorrow at the time of Christ's dying. For it belonged to the nature of all things to know he was their God, since in him stood their whole strength. When he failed, it was only natural that they must

---

[30] 'a substance of kind love': Julian is making a bold and original connection between our kind or human nature which Christ receives from his mother and accepts as his own and our loving response to his incarnation that is grounded in kind and 'continued by grace'. As mother, Mary has a unique compassion for his suffering; yet through the same kin(d)ship with him, we too have a similar 'kind love' that is perfected by grace.

fail with him, as far as they might, sorrowing at his pains. And so too, those that were his friends suffered for their love of him. And in general, everyone – even those who knew him not – suffered as they felt the loss of the comfort from God's inner keeping.

I will mention just two people in particular: Pilate and Dionysius of France[31] who was then a pagan. When he saw signs of sorrow and dreadful marvels happening at that time, he said: 'Either the world has come to an end, or else he that has made all nature is suffering.' Because of this he wrote on an altar: 'This is the altar of the unknown God.'

The good God that made the planets and all the elements to work for the benefit of all humanity, be they blessed or cursed, withdrew at this time from them both; so that even those who could not recognize him were in sorrow at that time. And so our Lord was made nothing for us, and in this way we all stand as nothing with him; and shall do until we come to his bliss, as I shall tell later.

19

A T this time, I wanted to look away from the cross, yet I dared not do so. For I knew well that all the while I beheld the cross, I was sure and safe; therefore I determined not to put my soul in peril, for without the cross there was no safeguard from the horror of fiends.

---

[31] Julian names St Denys, patron of France, before history had perhaps sorted out three people of this name: Dionysius the Areopagite, whom Paul names in this same context, the pagan instinctively feeling Christ's death; St Denys (c. 250), Bishop of Paris and martyr, one of the seven bishops sent to convert Gaul; and Dionysius the Pseudo-Areopagite whose writings linked Neoplatonism to Christianity, thereby fathering mystical theology. Julian appears to confuse the first two.

Then a suggestion came to mind, just like a friend inviting me: 'Look up to heaven, to his Father.' And then I was sure in my faith that there was nothing between the cross and heaven that could draw me aside. Either I must look up or else answer for myself. I did so inwardly with every power in my soul, saying: 'No, I may not, for you are my heaven.' I said this because I would not look up; for I had rather borne that pain till Doomsday than come to heaven other than by him. For I know well enough that since it was he who bound me so sore, then would he unbind me as and when he willed.

Thus I was taught to choose Jesus to be my heaven, whom at that time I could only see in pain. Yet I desired no other heaven than Jesus; and he shall be my bliss when I come there. And ever since then, this has always been my comfort, that, by his grace, I chose Jesus to be my heaven throughout this time of passion and of sorrow. And that lesson has served me that I should do so evermore, choosing only Jesus for my heaven in weal and woe. And though, wretch as I am, I repented my prayer (I said before that if I had known what this pain would mean, I would have been unwilling to have prayed for it), here I saw clearly that it was only the complaining weak flesh without assent of the soul; and in this God assigns no blame. Repenting and deliberate choice are two separate things, and I felt them both at the same time; for they belong to two different aspects, the outward and the inner.[32] The outward part is our mortal flesh which is presently in pain and woe, and will always be in this life; it was this that weighed on me heavily at this time. This part, it was, repented. The inner part is a high and blissful life all at peace and kept in love; and this was felt more secretly; and within this part I did choose Jesus to be my heaven mightily, wisely and with all my will. And in this I saw in truth that the inward part is master and

---

32 The first statement of Julian's distinction between our substance and our sensuality: the inner will 'at peace and kept in love' draws the outer by grace. This is developed further in chapters 37 and 55.

lord over the outer, neither regarding nor taking heed to it, but all the effort of will is set steadfastly to join with our Lord Jesus. I was not shown that the outer should draw the inner to assent; but that the inner draws the outer by grace, and both will be oned in bliss without end by the power of Christ: this was I shown.

20

ND thus I saw our Lord Jesus lingering a long while; for the unity with the Godhead gave strength to the manhood to suffer in love more than anyone else might suffer. By that I mean not only more pain than anyone at all might suffer, but also that he suffered more pain than the whole of humanity from the first to the last day of salvation, considering the worth of this highest, most honourable king and his shameful, cruel and painful death. For he that is highest and most worthy was completely humiliated and utterly despised. Indeed the highest point in the passion is to think and know who it is that suffered.

And in this he brought to mind, in part, the height and nobility of the glorious Godhead and with it the preciousness and tenderness of the blessed body, which are together as one, as well as the loathing for pain that belongs to our nature. For inasmuch as he was most tender and clean, so also was he most strong and mighty to suffer; for all humankind's sin that shall be saved did he suffer; and he saw and grieved with us for every human sorrow and desolation, from his kindness* and love. And as much as our Lady sorrowed for his pains, so too did he grieve in kind[33] for her sorrow, and more than her,

---

33 kind: i.e. nature. Being human with us, he was joined in our grief. Cf. ch. 18.

since his sweet manhood was so much worthier by comparison. He suffered for us just as long it was possible for him to suffer;[34] but now he is risen up, he no longer suffers; yet still he suffers with us.

I beheld all this, by his grace, and saw how his love for our soul is so strong that he chose firmly with great resolve to suffer all mildly, making light of what he paid. Thus the soul touched by this grace beholds the very truth: that the pains of Christ's passion pass all pain. Yet I say these pains shall be turned into everlasting great joys by virtue of Christ's passion.

21

I wanted him most earnestly to die for I thought I saw his body was quite dead. But then I realized my mistake, that this was not so. For at the very moment when it appeared to me that life could not be sustained and that the vision must of necessity come to an end, suddenly, as I still looked at the cross, I saw that his blessed face had changed. It was this change that at once affected me: for I was now as glad and happy as could be. Our Lord brought to mind the words: 'Where now is there any point in the pain or in your grief?' In my new-found joy, I saw that in this life, in our Lord's plan, we are with him on his cross, dying with him in our pains and passion; when of a sudden his face will change in our sight, and then we will be with him in heaven. There will be no time between one state and the other: suddenly we will be brought to his joy. This is what he meant by the words: 'Where now is there any point in the pain or your grief?' Then we shall be full of bliss.

I saw the truth in this that if he were to show himself to us

---

[34] *for as long as he was passible, he suffryd for us*: a word knot that plays with passible and possible.

now, no pain imaginable that could fall our way on earth or elsewhere would trouble us, for everything would be to our joy and happiness. But instead he offers us some measure of the passion that he himself suffered in his own life. We are afflicted by his own cross and so we suffer with him, as is our human lot. And his reason for suffering in this way? He wants of his goodness to make us heirs with him in his bliss. As our reward for the little pain we suffer here, we will know God himself without end which otherwise we might never have. And the greater are our pains with him on his cross, the greater will be our reward with him when we come into his kingdom.

THE NINTH SHOWING

22

The working of the Father is this: he gives his Son, Jesus Christ, a prize —
we are his prize, we are his crown.

THEN our good Lord asked me: 'Are you pleased I suffered for you?' I said: 'Yes, dear Lord, in your mercy: yes, good Lord, bless you always.' Then our good Lord Jesus replied: 'If you are pleased, then I too am pleased. This is my joy, my bliss, my endless liking that I was ever able to suffer for you. For truly, if I could have suffered more, I would have suffered more.'

As I attended to this, my understanding was lifted into heaven; where I saw three heavens. Seeing them, I wondered at it all, saying: 'I see three heavens, each one belonging to the blessed manhood of Christ; none is greater, none is less: yet all are of equal blessedness.' In the first heaven, Christ showed me his Father – not in bodily vision, but in his property and in his working, that is to say, I saw in Christ that his Father is.

The working of the Father is this: he gives his Son, Jesus

Christ, a prize. This gift and prize is so great a reward to Jesus, that his Father could give him none better or more pleasing to him. The first heaven is his rewarding his Father (it was shown like heaven since it was so full of blessedness). For the Father is greatly pleased with everything Jesus has done towards our salvation. So that we are not merely his by his buying, but, by the courteous gift of the Father, we are equally his happiness, we are his prize, we are his crown.

This singular marvel, that we could be his crown, gave me utter delight: what I am saying is that this means so much to Jesus that all the labour of his passion, his cruel and shameful death, is as nothing to him.

These were his very words: 'If I could suffer more, I would suffer more.' I saw clearly that he would be willing to die as often as was needed; his love would drive him on till he has done it. I beheld with great diligence to learn how many times he would have died if he might; but the numbers were so great that it was too much for me and I lost count. Yet if he had died all those times, because of his great love he would still have counted it as nothing. Since he is man, sweet Jesus may only suffer once, yet of his goodness he would do so again and again, as if each day he would be in travail once more. And yet supposing, to show me his love, he were to make new heavens and new earths, it would mean little to me, for he might do so every day simply by saying the word. But for him to die for my love, so often that a creature loses count, that is the highest offer that our Lord God could make for a human soul, in my eyes.

This then is what he means: 'How can there be anything I would not do for love of you? I might and would do all else besides, since I would gladly die of your love so often, ignoring all my hard pains.'

And now as I thought about his blessed passion, I began also to understand about the second heaven: for his love that brought him to suffer exceeds his pain as much as heaven is above the earth. For although the pain was surely noble, precious and honourable, it was achieved by the work of his love in time. But this same love was without beginning; it is now and it will be without end. This was the love that prompted him to tell me, 'If I could suffer more, I would suffer more.' He did not say 'if I had to suffer more', but 'if I could suffer more'; whether it were necessary or not.

This deed God worked to achieve our salvation and it was done to perfection, as only God could devise. In our salvation, Christ won every honour. I knew this because of the joy that was his: for that bliss would not have been perfect had his deed fallen short in any way.

23

I was shown three heavens in these words he spoke: 'This is my joy, my happiness, my endless liking.' These were as follows: for the joy, I understood the Father's good pleasure; for the happiness, the honour given to the Son; and for the endless liking, the Holy Spirit. The Father is pleased, the Son is honoured and the Holy Spirit rests content – without end.

Now I will tell of the third heaven which I saw in the passion, namely the joy and the happiness that makes him like it. Our courteous Lord showed me his passion five different ways: the first is the bleeding of his head; the second, the discolouring of his blessed face; the third is the plentiful bleeding of the body when it was scourged; the fourth, the deep dying. These four were shown as the pains of his passion. The fifth is what was shown me as the joy and bliss of his passion. For God wants us to share in his pleasure at our salvation, taking comfort and strength that we have been saved. He wants our soul to be busy at this task, merrily cheered by his grace. For we are his bliss; in us he takes his liking without end and so shall we in him, with his grace. And everything he does, has done or will do for us is no cost or charge to him, save only when he died in our humanity. And all this began at the sweet Incarnation, lasting to the day when he rose again on Easter day; this was the extent and the reckoning of the work that made our redemption come about. In this work he finds his endless joy, as has already been said.

Jesus wants us to take to heed of all the bliss that is in the blessed Trinity for our salvation; and that we desire to have as much liking in spirit, with his grace, as is already said: that is to say, the liking we take in our salvation should be similar to Christ's own joy, so far as it is possible on this earth. All the Trinity worked together in the passion of Christ, affording us the generous power of his abundant grace. While it was only he, Mary's Son, that suffered, yet all the Trinity rejoice in it without end. This much I recognized in the saying: 'Are you well pleased that I suffered?' and again when Christ said: 'If you are pleased, then I too am pleased'; as if he would say: 'It is joy and liking enough to know you feel like this; I ask nothing more of my labours than that I can pay you generously.'

This reminded me what marks out the glad giver. A glad giver takes but little heed of what he gives; for the only thing that matters is to please the person to whom he gives. And so if the person receives his gift gladly and with gratitude, the courteous giver has no further thought as to what his task has cost, since he knows he has pleased and satisfied his lover. This was shown me clearly and without stint.

Think also wisely of the greatness of this word 'ever'[35]: it contains high wisdom about Christ's love for our salvation and all the many joys that flow from his passion. Firstly how glad he is that he has done the deed once for all and need suffer no more. Again, by his deed he has bought us from the pains of hell; yet more, he has brought us all the way to heaven where he will make us his crown to be his endless bliss.

---

[35] 'This is my joy, my bliss, my endless liking that I was *ever* able to suffer for you' (ch.22).

24

'He showed a place inviting fair and large enough for all that
shall be saved to rest in peace and love ... "Lo, how I loved you ...".'
A showing of his heart, broken in two.

WITH joyful face our good Lord looked down at his side and I was invited by his tender gaze to ponder this wound. For there within, he showed a place that was inviting fair; and large enough it was to offer refuge for all who will be saved, there to find their rest in peace and love. And with this sweet beholding he brought to mind his most dear blood and the precious water which he let pour from his side, all of his love. And looking with him, I realized that his heart was indeed broken in two. Now with his tender look he revealed something of God's inner bliss, as my soul was led in some measure to know his never-ending love, flowing from before time, to the present and for all eternity. And with this our good Lord gently spoke: 'Lo, how I loved you.' It was as if he had said: 'My darling, behold and see your Lord, and your God, who is your Maker and your endless joy; see what liking and bliss I have in your salvation, and for my love enjoy now with me.' To understand to the full these words of his, 'See how I love you', it was as if he were to say: 'Lo how I loved you. Behold and see that I loved you so much that before ever I died for you, I would die for you; and now I have died for you and willingly suffered all that I may. And now is all my bitter pain and all my hard travail turned into endless joy and bliss to me and to you. How could you pray anything of me that I like that I would not fully grant? For my liking is your holiness and your endless joy and your bliss with me.'

This is the understanding, as simply as I can say, of this

blessed word: 'Lo, how I loved you.' Our good Lord showed us as much to make us glad and merry.

THE ELEVENTH SHOWING

25

'Will you see her?'
Three spiritual visions of our Lady.

HIS face still full of mirth and joy, our Lord now looked down to his right side, and I was reminded where our Lady stood all the while he suffered on his cross. And he said: 'Will you see her?' And in this sweet word, it was as if he said: 'Surely you want to see my blessed Mother; for next to me, she is the highest joy I could show you. Of all my dear creatures, it is she that gives me most delight and honour – to see her is a heart's desire.'

Because of his own special and exalted love that he holds for his blessed Mother, our Lady Saint Mary, he showed her full of joy and happiness. This is what he meant, as if to say: 'Will you see how I love her, so that you may share the joy I have in her and she in me?' And also, in order that this sweet word be better understood, our Lord God speaks to all those who shall be saved as to one person, as though he had said: 'Will you see in her how you are loved? It was for love of you that I made her so high, so noble, so worthy. This pleases me, and I would that it please you.'

After his own self, she is the most blissful sight. Yet just because of that, I am not taught that I should long to see her bodily presence while I am here, but simply the good virtues of her holy soul – her truth, her wisdom and her love. Whereby I may learn to know myself and reverently dread my God. And when our good Lord had showed this and spoke these words, 'Will you see her?' I answered saying: 'Yes, dear Lord, in your mercy: yes, good Lord, if it be your will.' Oftentimes I prayed for this, and I thought that I wanted to see her in bodily presence, but I never saw her so. But in this saying of Jesus I was shown her in a spiritual way. Whereas before I had seen her little and simple, now he showed her high and noble and glorious, more pleasing to him than any other creature. And he made it known that anyone who loves him should also love her, even in the same way as he loves her and she loves him. As if to make this plain, I was shown an example: if a man loves someone very dearly, more than any other, he will wish everyone to love and esteem that person in the same way. And in the words that Jesus spoke, 'Will you see her?', this seemed to me the most loving way he could tell me how much he loved her, together with the spiritual vision of her I was given. Our Lord showed me no one else apart from her; in all I saw her three times. The first as a maiden when she first conceived; the second when she mourned beneath the cross; and third, as she now is, full of liking, joy and honour.

THE TWELFTH SHOWING

26

'I it am ...'

AFTER this our Lord revealed himself even more glorified, as far as I may tell, than I had seen before. And then I knew that our soul will never be at rest until it comes into him: then we will know him as our true life and be filled with his joy, happiness and his courteous homeliness.

And now our Lord repeated many times:

I it am, I it am;
I it am that is highest;

I it am that you love;
I it am that you like;
I it am that you serve;
I it am that you long for;
I it am that you desire;
I it am that you mean;
I it am that is all;
I it am that holy Church preaches and teaches you;
I it am that showed myself to you here.'[36]

His words were so many that I could never hope to take them all in, past my wit and my understanding; for they are the highest of all words I know. What they mean I cannot say: except that, when I saw them in the showings, they filled me with such joy that my heart and soul overflowed. Therefore the words may not be declared here, yet everyone may receive them, coming to our Lord's meaning with love and understanding insofar as God gives them grace.

THE THIRTEENTH SHOWING

27

'"Sin is necessary, but all shall be well.
All shall be well; and all manner of thing shall be well."
This was said so tenderly, without blame of any kind
towards me or to anybody else.'

THEN our Lord took my mind back to the longing I had for him before. And I saw that nothing had held me back save sin; and I beheld the same thing in us all. And I thought that if it were not for sin, we should all have been

---

[36] When God first called Moses, he spoke his name as 'I Am who I Am' (Exodus 3.14).

clean and in our Lord's liking, as when he made us. And so it was, that in my folly, before this time I would often wonder why in God's great foresight and wisdom, sin had not been forestalled in its beginning; for then, thought I, all should be well. These thoughts were hard to forsake and I turned them over endlessly with no proper reason or discretion until they made me mourn and sorrow. But Jesus, who in this vision had informed me of all that I needed, answered with these words saying:

'Sin is necessary, but all shall be well.
All shall be well; and all manner of thing shall be well.'

In this naked word 'sin' our Lord brought to mind in general everything that is not good, and the shameful despising, the utter humiliation that he bore for us in this life, and his dying and the many pains that all his creatures also suffer; both in spirit and body – for we all share in his humiliation, that way we follow our master Jesus until we are fully purged; that is to say, until we be fully rid of our mortal flesh and of all our inward affections which are not true and good. Such was my beholding, along with all the pains that ever were or ever shall be; yet compared to all these, I understood that the passion of Christ was the most pain by far. But all this was shown in a touch and then it swiftly passed over into comfort; our Lord never meant to terrify a soul with such an ugly sight.

But all this while, I never once saw sin. For I believe it has neither manner of substance nor part of being, and it would not even be known save for the pain it causes. Yet this pain is indeed something, as I see it, for it purges and makes us know ourself as we ask for mercy, while the passion of our Lord comforts us against all this, all according to his blessed will. And our good Lord, with all the tender love he has for all those that shall be saved, comforts readily and sweetly, for thus is his meaning: 'It is true that sin is the cause of all this pain, but all shall be well, and all shall be well, and all manner of thing shall be well.' This was said so tenderly, without blame of any kind towards me or to anybody else. Therefore it would be a great unkindness to wonder or complain of sin to God, since he puts no blame on me.

As he spoke these words, I saw they held a marvellous secret hid in God that he will only make known in heaven. Then shall we see why he allowed sin to come; and that will all add to our everlasting joy.

28

THUS I saw how Christ has compassion on us because of sin. And just as before, in the passion of Christ, I was filled full of pain and compassion, so now I was filled in a lesser way with compassion for all my fellow Christians – full well he loves those people that shall be saved. Yet God's servants, that is to say holy Church, shall be shaken in sorrow and anguish and tribulation in this world, just as people shake a cloth in the wind.[37]

But our Lord answered in this way: 'I shall make a great thing of this in heaven, a thing of endless honour and everlasting joy.' Then I saw why it was that our Lord rejoices in the tribulations of his servants, yet always with pity and compassion. In order to bring them to bliss, he lays on those that he loves something which, though nothing is lost in his sight, is the way they are humbled and despised in this world, scorned, mocked and cast aside. He does this to prevent them taking any harm from the pomp and vainglory of this wretched life and to make the way ready for them to come to heaven, raising them to his bliss that will last without end. For he says: 'I will

---

[37] This image complements Julian's showing of Christ hanging in the drying, bitter wind (ch. 16); for he is in his Church as it is 'shaken in sorrow and anguish and tribulation'.

49

wholly break you of your vain affections and your vicious pride; and after that I shall gather you and make you meek and mild, clean and holy by oneing you to me.' Then I saw that each time we have kind compassion and charity for our fellow Christian, that is Christ in him. For the same emptying of self that he showed in his passion is to be seen again here in this compassion.

And in this our Lord showed two ways of understanding his meaning. One was the bliss to which we are to be brought and how he wants us to rejoice in it. The other is the comfort in our present pain by our knowing that it will all be turned to honour and our gain by virtue of his passion; and we should know too that we never suffer alone but with him whom we should see as our ground; also when we see his own pains and his own emptying, this so far exceeds anything we might suffer as to pass beyond our understanding.

Beholding this much, we will be saved from grumbling or complaint in time of pain. And though we see truly that our sins deserve it, yet his love excuses us; and with his great courtesy he does away with all our blame, beholding us with compassion and pity like children who are innocent whom he can never reject.

29

BUT I stood beholding this in general, with sorrow and mourning, and spoke thus to our Lord, fully meaning it with great dread: 'Ah! good Lord, how can all be well, since such great harm has come by sin to all your creatures?' What I wanted, as much as I dared, was some more open saying which could settle my dismay. And at this, our Lord answered most meekly and with full* lovely look. He showed me that Adam's sin was the greatest harm that was ever done or ever shall be, until the world ends; and he also showed that this is clearly known in all the holy Church on earth. But more, he taught me that I should recognize his glorious remedy. For the work of his re-making is more pleasing to God and honours humankind's salvation more, without comparison, than any harm that ever came from Adam's sin. What our blessed Lord means by this teaching, what we should take to heart, is this: 'Seeing that I have made well the greatest harm, I want you to know that I shall make well all that is less.'

30

HE gave me to understand there are two parts to his truth. One part is our Saviour and our salvation; this blessed part is open, clear and fair, as well as light and plenteous. For all humankind of good will that are and shall be are comprehended in this part. This is how we are bound in by God and drawn to him, how we are counselled and taught both inwardly by the Holy Spirit and outwardly by holy Church, both by the same grace. Our Lord wants us to make this our business, enjoying in him, just as he enjoys us.[38] The more plentifully we accept this joy, with reverence and meekness, the more thanks we deserve of him and the more progress we ourselves make. Thus may we come to see that it is our lot to enjoy our Lord.

Yet the other part is hidden and closed to us, namely, all that is beyond our own salvation. For this belongs to our Lord's secret counsel: the royal lordship of God has his own privy counsel in peace. And for obedience and due reverence, it is not his servant's place to want to know this counsel. But our Lord

---

[38] 'Rejoice in the Lord always; I repeat, rejoice' (Philippians 4.4). The Carthusians, when they write a letter, will sign off 'Peace & Joy'.

has pity and understands us when some of his creatures busy themselves in this way. Yet I am sure that, if we knew how much we would please him and save ourselves trouble by leaving it alone, we would do so.[39] The saints in heaven wish to know nothing save what our Lord would show them, since their love and desire is ruled only by the will of our Lord. And so we ought to will just as they do, wishing for none other than the will of our Lord – for we are all one in God's meaning. And here I was taught that we should trust and find joy only in our blessed Saviour Jesus for all things.

31

'I may ... I can ... I will ... I shall make all things well ...'

IT was in this way that our good Lord answered all the questions and doubts I might make, comforting me greatly with these words:

'I may make all thing well; I can make all thing well, and I will make all thing well, and I shall make all thing well; and you shall see for yourself that all manner of thing shall be well.'

When he says 'I may', I understand it to mean the Father; and as he says 'I can', I understand the Son; and where he says 'I will', I understand the Holy Spirit; and where he says 'I shall', I understand the unity of the Trinity, three Persons and one truth; and where he says 'You shall see for yourself', I understand the union of all humankind that shall be saved into the blessed Trinity.

---

39 Julian's admonition is not merely to individuals who ask questions but to those in authority, some of whom are fond of giving cast-iron answers and thereby erecting what has been called the Church of boxes, each with its own tidy label.

And in these five words God wills that we be enclosed in rest and peace: so shall the thirst of Christ's spirit be quenched; for this is his spiritual thirst – the love-longing that lasts and will ever last till we see that sight on Doomsday. For we that shall be saved and shall be Christ's joy and his bliss, some are still here, some are yet to come and so some shall be alive on that very day. This then is his thirst, a love-longing to have us all together and whole in him to be his bliss, this is what I see. For now we are not fully whole in him as we shall be then.

For we know by faith what was also shown in all this, that Christ Jesus is both God and man. As regards the Godhead, he is himself the highest bliss and was from without beginning and shall be thus without end; the same bliss can never be increased nor diminished in himself. All this was shown most plainly in every showing but most especially in the twelfth where he says: 'I am that is highest.'

And as regards Christ's humanity (again we know by our faith and it is shown here), by virtue of the Godhead, out of love for us and in order to bring us to his bliss, he suffered pains and his passion and then he died; these are the works of Christ's manhood in which he finds his joy. This was contained and shown in the ninth revelation where he says: 'This is my joy, my happiness, my endless liking, that I was able to suffer for you.' This is the blessedness of Christ's works; this his meaning when he says in the same showing that we are his happiness, we are his prize, we are his honour, we are his crown. With regard to Christ as our head, he is already glorified and impassible; yet as regards his body in which all we his members are knit, he is not yet fully glorified or impassible; for the same desire and thirst that he had upon the cross – which desire, longing and thirst was his, as I see it, from without beginning – the same he has now and will have until that time comes when the last soul to be saved comes up to join him in his bliss; for as truly as there is a property in God of compassion and pity, so truly there is in God a property of thirst and longing. And because of the virtue of this longing of

Christ, we in turn long for him, for without it no soul would come to heaven.

And this property of longing and of thirst comes from the endless goodness of God, just as the property of pity is from his endless goodness. Though longing and pity are two different properties, as I see it; and in this stands the point of the spiritual thirst, which will last in him as long as we are in need, so as to draw us up to his bliss. And all this was in the vision of compassion which shall be made plain on Doomsday.

And this is why he has pity and compassion on us, for he longs to have us, but his wisdom and his love do not allow the end to come until the best time.

32

Developing the theme, 'all things shall be well':
still aware of the devastating effects of sin, Julian is told of
a great deed that will be done at the last by which
'he will make well all that is not well'.

AT one time our good Lord said: 'All thing shall be well'; and another time he said: 'You shall see for yourself that all manner of thing shall be well'; and in these two things this soul took separate understandings.

One was this: that he wishes us to know that not only does he take heed of noble things and the greatest, but he also attends to little and small, to low and simple, as much to one as to the other. This is his meaning when he said: 'All manner of things shall be well'; for he wants us to know that the least thing will not be forgotten.

Another understanding is this: that there are evil deeds done that we know of, when such great harm is taken that it seems to us that it were impossible that they should ever come to a good end. And we look upon this with sorrow and mourning, so that we are unable to rest in the blessed contemplation of God as we ought. And the cause is that the working of our reason here and now is so blind, so low and simple that we cannot know the high, marvellous wisdom, the might and goodness of the blessed Trinity. This is his meaning when he says: 'You shall see for yourself that all manner of thing shall be well', as if he had said: 'Take heed now in faith and trust, and at the last end you will see it truly in the fullness of joy.'

And so in these same five sayings that were said before: 'I may make all things well' etc., I understand a great comfort in all the works of our Lord God that are yet to come. There is a deed which the blessed Trinity shall do on the last day, as I see it, and when that deed shall be and how it shall be done is not known to any creatures that are beneath Christ; and so it shall be until it is done. And why he wants us to know this is that he wishes that we be more at ease in our soul and at peace in his love, disregarding all tempests that might keep us from truth but only enjoying in him.

This is the great deed that God has ordained from without beginning, treasured and hidden in his blissful breast, known only to himself, the deed by which he will make all things well. For just as the blessed Trinity made all things from nothing, even so the same blessed Trinity shall make well all that is not well. And in this sight I marvelled greatly and beheld our faith and I began to think as follows: our faith is grounded in God's word, and it belongs to our faith that we believe that God's word shall be kept in all things. Now one point of our faith is that many shall be damned – such as the angels that fell from heaven on account of their pride and are now fiends; or again a person here on earth who dies without the faith of holy Church, that is to say, those heathen people and also anyone that, having been a Christian, lives an unchristian life and comes to die out of charity – all these shall be condemned to hell without end, for so holy Church teaches me to believe. And thinking about all this, I thought it was impossible that all manner of things should be well as our Lord showed me at this time. And as for the difficulty contained in this showing, I had no answer from our Lord but this: 'What is impossible to you, is not impossible to me. I shall keep my word in all things, and I shall make all things well.'

Thus I was taught by the grace of God that I should hold myself steadfastly in the faith as I had understood all along, and I should thereby solemnly believe that all things shall be well just as our Lord showed me at that time. For this is the great deed that our Lord shall do, and by this deed he will keep his word in everything, and he will make well all that is not well.

And how it shall be done, there is no creature beneath Christ that knows or shall know until the time it is done. This is the understanding I took of our Lord's meaning at this time.

33

AND yet in this I desired, as far as I dared, that I might have had full sight of hell and purgatory. Not that it was in my mind to question anything that belongs to our faith – for I steadfastly believed that hell and purgatory exist for that very same purpose that holy Church teaches. But my intention was that I might recognize and understand all things belonging to my faith and so come to live more pleasing to God as well as making progress in myself.

But in spite of my desire, I could see nothing save only what I have already set down in the fifth showing, where I saw that the devil is confounded by God and endlessly damned. And I saw in the same understanding that all creatures that are of the devil's sort in this life and end it the same, no more mention is made of them before God and his holy ones any more than there is of the devil – notwithstanding that they be of the human race, whether Christian or no. Although the revelation treated of goodness, with little mention of evil, yet I was not drawn away by it from any single detail of the faith that holy Church teaches me to hold. For I had sight of the passion of Christ in various showings, namely in the first and second, in the fifth and the eighth, as I have already said; and although I had in part some feeling for the sorrow which our Lady and his true friends felt when they saw him in pain, yet I saw no specific mention at all of the Jews who had put him to death. Yet I know in my faith that they were cursed and damned without end, saving those who were converted by grace.

And I was strengthened and taught in general to keep my faith in every detail and in all I had understood before, hoping in this way that I was held in the mercy and grace of God, only wishing and praying in my every intention that I might continue in such way to my life's end. And it is God's will that we have great regard for all his deeds that he has done, but all the while we should leave aside our curiosity as to what that great deed shall be. For we should seek to be like our brethren the saints in heaven who want nothing but the will of God; in this way we will delight only in God and be equally rewarded whether he shows himself or pleases to remain hidden. For truly I saw our Lord's meaning: the more we busy ourselves to know his secrets now in this, now in the other, the further shall we be from knowing them.

34

OUR Lord showed two kind of secrets: one is the great secret with all the hidden details belonging to it, and these kinds of secrets he wants us to know are hidden until the time comes when he will reveal them clearly to us. The other are secrets he will open and make known to us; and these, he wants us to know, it is his will that we know. These are secrets to us not only because such is his will, but they are also secret on account of our own blindness and our ignorance; and on account of this he has great pity, and accordingly he himself will make them more clear to us so that we may know him and love him and hold fast to him. For all that it is expedient for us to grasp and to know, our Lord himself will courteously show us – that is this[40] – together with all the preaching and teaching of the holy Church. For it is his holy Church; he is the ground, he is the substance, he is the teaching, he is the teacher, he is the taught,[41] he is the reward for which every human soul searches; this much is known and shall be known by every soul to whom the Holy Spirit speaks. I truly hope that he will quicken[42] all those that seek this, for they are seeking God.

All this that I say now, and more that I will add later, is a comfort against sin; for in the third showing when I saw how God does all that is done, I saw no sin, for I saw then that all is well. But it was when God showed me sin, then did he say: 'All shall be well.'

---

[40] It is not clear to what 'this' refers: it could be all those secondary secrets pertaining to our own salvation or possibly the revelations themselves. It is curious to find Julian, for all her sixteen showings, still busy to find more. But she herself warns against too much 'busyness' and offers instead the treasures of the Church's teachings. For no private revelation can say more than God has already revealed to his Church.

[41] leryd: learned, the (one) taught: a disputed reading that has finally been convincingly argued by Marion Glasscoe. To say of Christ that he is both teacher, teaching and taught throws fresh light on Newman's theory of the development of doctrine. We are familiar with the boy Christ learning in the Temple: here the implication is that he is still being taught within his Church.

[42] spedyn: i.e. speed them on their way, enable them.

35

AND after God almighty had shown me his goodness so generously and fully, I desired to learn about a certain person that I loved, whether they would persevere in godly living, which I hoped by God's grace was begun. And in this particular desire, it seemed to me that I took harm, since I was shown nothing at this time. And then I was answered in my understanding, as if by a friend's voice: 'Take it in general, having regard to the courtesy of the Lord God who showed it to you; for it does more honour to God to behold him in everything than in any special thing.'

I saw the sense of this and was thereby taught that God is honoured more by knowing all things in general than by taking delight in any one thing in particular.[43] And if I were to follow the wisdom of this teaching, I should not only be glad for nothing in particular, nor should I be greatly put out at anything that might take place, for 'All shall be well'. And the fullness of joy is to behold God in everything that happens; for by the same blessed might, wisdom and love that he made everything, to the same end our good Lord continually leads it, and he himself shall bring it about; and in due time we will see it. And the ground of all this was shown in the first revelation and more clearly in the third where it says: 'I saw God in a point.'

All that our Lord does is right-full,[44] and what he permits to occur is always praiseworthy. And in these two is comprehended good and evil; for all that is good our Lord does, and that which is evil he permits. I am not saying that evil is praiseworthy, but I say that our Lord God's suffering it is praise-

---

[43] Julian is addressing here the contemplative's dilemma of petitioning God for a single cause as distinct from the totality of all his works. She would seem to say that in God's eyes each individual's cause is regarded equally and as a whole.

[44] See ch. 11, footnote 24.

worthy; whereby his goodness shall be known without end, together with his marvellous meekness and mildness, in the workings of his mercy and grace. Rightfulness is when something is so good that it may not be better than it is; and God himself is most rightfulness and his works are rightfully done as they are ordained from without beginning by his high might, his high wisdom and his high goodness. And right as he ordained it to the best, right so he works continually and leads it to the same end; therefore he is always pleased with himself and with all his works.

And to behold[45] this blessed harmony gives great comfort to a soul that is held in grace. All the souls that shall be saved forever in heaven are made rightful in God's sight by his own goodness; and in his rightfulness we are continually and marvellously kept, above all creatures.[46]

Mercy is a working that comes from the goodness of God, and it shall last in its working all the while sin is suffered to pursue the rightful soul. And when sin is no more permitted to pursue, then shall the working of mercy cease. And then shall we be brought to rightfulness where we will stand without end. For it is only by his sufferance we fall; yet in his blessed love we are kept with his might and wisdom; and by his mercy and grace we are raised to manifold more joys. And thus in rightfulness and in mercy he will be known and loved, now and without end. And the soul that wisely beholds it in grace is well pleased with both, and its joy shall last without end.

---

[45] 'Beholding' – to repeat – is used here to say more than the word can bear: 'survey with still enjoyment'. Perhaps the mental image to be conjured is a boy gazing with adoration across the room at the girl he knows loves him and she returning his glance with reciprocal love.

[46] Let us take the image of a skylark singing above a meadow: perfection, declares the poet. And Julian would agree, for God made the skylark so it cannot help but sing the praises of God to perfection. This illustrates Julian's problem of sin by which our kind (nature) has offended God. But she now has the revelation concerning 'the great deed to come'.

36

OUR Lord God showed that a deed shall be done and he himself shall do it; while I shall do nothing but sin, yet my sin will not prevent the work of his goodness.

This deed shall be most honourable, marvellous and generous: I saw that beholding this is sublime joy for a fearful soul, which, kindly by grace, always desires God's will. This deed shall be begun here, and it shall bring honour to God and much reward to his lovers on earth. And as soon as we reach heaven, then shall we see its marvellous joy in full. It will continue to work thus until the last day; yet the honour and the happiness that belongs to it shall last before God and his holy ones without end. Thus was this deed seen and understood according to our Lord's meaning; and he showed it so that we may find joy in him and in all his works.

When I saw his showing continued, I understood that it stood for a great thing that was to come. God showed that he himself would do it, and the nature of his deed has already been described. For he showed it most blissfully, meaning me to take it wisely, trusting him in faith. But what this deed should be, that was kept hidden from me. And here I saw he wants us not to fear to know those things he shows us, for that is why he shows them, so that we may know them. And in this knowledge he wants us to love, like and find joy in him, without any end. As a measure of his great love for us, he shows us all that is honest and to our purpose for the moment; and even the things that he chooses to keep from us now, he shows them hid so that we may learn and understand that we shall see it clearly in his endless bliss.

So must we be glad in him for all that he shows and all that he hides; and if we do so obediently and meekly, we shall find great peace of heart and because of it we will earn his endless thanks. Here are how his words should be taken: the deed shall be done for me – that is to say humankind in general, or rather, all who are to be save – it is to be honourable, marvellous and generous and God himself will do it. And this shall be the highest joy that may be, to witness the deed that God himself will do: while all human beings may do is sin.

This is our Lord's meaning, as if he would say: 'Behold and see. Here you have matter for meekness; here is your message of love; here is the way to forget yourself; here is your reason to find your joy in me; see my love and find your joy in me, for more than anything this pleases me most.'

And for as long as we live, whenever in our foolishness we take up with the wicked, our Lord tenderly touches us, calls us delightfully, saying in our soul: 'My dearest child, let go of all this you love. Turn to me, for I am enough for you: take your joy in your Saviour and in your salvation.' That this is how our Lord is working in us, I am sure; the soul made aware by grace will see and feel this. And although it is true that this deed should be understood of all humanity in general, yet it does not exclude the individual; for what our good Lord wills to do for each of his poor creatures, I do not now know. But this deed and the other I have mentioned, they are not the same but two different deeds. But this deed shall be done the sooner – when each of us comes to heaven; and it may also be known here in some part to whom our Lord reveals it. But the great deed that has already been named will never be known in heaven nor on earth until the time that it is done.

Furthermore, he gave special understanding and teaching of the purpose of miracles, as follows: 'It is known that in the past I have done miracles that were many and far-reaching, high and marvellous, praiseworthy and great; and as I did then, so I do now without ceasing and shall continue throughout the time that is to come.'

It is known that before miracles come sorrow and anguish and tribulation; this in order that we should come to know our own feebleness and the mischief into which we have fallen through sin; thus humbled, we come to fear God and call to him for help and grace. Miracles follow after that, token of the high might, wisdom and goodness of God; they show too his virtue and promise the joys of heaven so much as can be in this passing life; and in this way our faith is strengthened, our hope and charity increased. For these reasons he is pleased to be known and honoured in miracles.

His meaning then is this: he wants us not to be brought too low by sorrow and the storms that befall us; for this is always the way before the miracle comes.

37

Julian begins to elaborate her teaching of the two wills —
a beastly, or lower will that is prone to sin and
a godly will in the higher part that does only good.

GOD brought to mind that I would sin; yet since my liking was on beholding him, I was not ready to attend to this showing. And our Lord most mercifully remained and gave me grace to listen to him. This was a show-ing that at first I took personally to myself, but then I was taught by all the grace and comfort that came after, as you shall see, to apply it to all my fellow Christians in general and not just to myself; so that although our Lord showed me I would sin, by me alone I understood everyone.

And at this, I was overcome with a soft fear; but our Lord responded with the words: 'I keep you full surely.' These words were spoken with more love and reassurance for my soul's keeping than I can say or ever tell. For although it was clear that I should sin, most surely was this comfort shown; so too was there the same sure promise of safe keeping for all my fel-low Christians.

What might make me love my fellow Christians more than to learn from God that he loves all the saved as if they were but one soul? For in every soul that shall be saved is a godly will that never assents to sin nor ever shall. Just as there is a beastly will in the lower part that can will no good, so is there a godly will in the higher part, and this will is so good that it may never will evil but only good. And accordingly we are what he loves and we always do his liking. Our Lord showed this by the wholeness of love in which we stand as one in his sight: yes, just this – he loves us now, while we are here, just as well as he will when we stand before his own blessed face. It is only the failing of love on our side that is the cause of all our travail.

38

GOD also showed that sin shall cause us no shame, but will even be accounted to our honour. For just as every sin is answered in reality by a particular pain, so for every sin that same soul is given joy by love. And as different sins are punished by various pains in accordance with their gravity, so will they be rewarded in heaven by joys that differ according to the pain and sorrow they caused that soul on earth. For the soul coming to heaven is precious to God, while the place itself is destined to reward us so fully that God in his goodness never permits sinful souls to come there without rewarding them for the pain they suffered by their sins. And this is made known without end while they are joyfully restored with overpassing honour.

This sight lifted my understanding up to heaven, and God made me merry as he reminded me of David and many others in the Old Law without number. While in the New Law, he brought to mind firstly Mary Magdalen, Peter and Paul, Thomas of India and St John of Beverley and many others[47] also without number: how they are known to the Church on earth by their sins, yet this is no shame on their part, rather is it turned to their honour. In this way our courteous Lord showed how it is with them here imperfectly, whereas in heaven it will be realized in full; for there the token of sin is transformed into the highest honour.

And our Lord in his familiarity and for our comfort showed St John of Beverley in his fullest glory above, and I was reminded that he is a near neighbour, someone we know. And God called him St John of Beverley, plainly, just as we do and this with a very glad, sweet expression showing that, in his sight, he is a very important saint in heaven, full of bliss and glory. And with this he made it clear how as a youth of tender age he was a beloved servant of God, one who loved and feared him very much; nevertheless God allowed him to fall, yet in his mercy he kept him from perishing and made sure that he lost no time at all. And afterwards God raised him to far greater grace because of the contrition and meekness he had in his life, so that in heaven God gave him manifold joys which outweigh any he might have had if he had not fallen.

And God shows this to be so on earth by the many miracles he does about his body all the time. And all this was to make us glad and merry in his love.

---

47 Thomas, the doubter, was by tradition the Apostle of India. Julian's showings took place on the eve of the feast day of John of Beverley (d. 721). First a monk at Whitby, then Bishop of Hexham, John was one of the most popular saints of Julian's day. (A little later, Henry V ascribed his victory at Agincourt to the saint.) It would appear common knowledge – yet the details are unknown today – that as bishop he retired to the Continent to live as a solitary, the customary penance to atone for a public sin. His tomb was a major place of pilgrimage where many miracles were worked.

39

SIN is the sharpest scourge which may smite any chosen soul. This scourge repeatedly flails both man and woman by which they are so reduced in their own sight that at times it seems to them they are only worthy to sink into hell. But then contrition takes hold of them and, at the touching of the Holy Spirit, all their bitterness changes into hope for God's mercy. Then their wounds begin to heal and the soul revives as it turns towards the life of holy Church.

The Holy Spirit leads them to confession,[48] gladly to reveal their sins in naked truth and with great sorrow and shame that God's fair image has been so besmirched. Then for each sin they are given a penance which their confessor lays upon them; and all this belongs to the practice of holy Church by the teaching of the Holy Spirit. This kind of meekness is most pleasing to God; and also all sickness of body that he may send, as well as sorrow and shame from without, that is to say the rebukes and despising of the world together with all manner of annoyance and temptation that will come their way, both bodily and spiritual.

Although it may seem to us that we are almost forsaken and cast away for our sins and that we deserve it all, yet our Lord keeps us as his most precious prize always. And because of the meekness that we hereby gain, we are raised up high in God's sight, by his grace, with such great contrition together with compassion and true longing for God. Then are the just suddenly delivered from sin and from pain and taken up to heavenly bliss where they join the company of the highest saints.

---

[48] Sacramental confession such as Julian describes was a once or twice a year event that would have filled the streets of Norwich at Lent and Advent as people came into the city to be shriven. It is far less common today even in the Roman Church. But the important essentials of her teaching remain: we must confess our sins, not bury them, bringing them to God for his merciful forgiveness. See her opening remarks that follow in ch. 40.

By contrition we are made clean, by compassion we are made ready, and by true longing for God we are made worthy of him. These three are means by which, as I understand, all souls come to heaven; that is to say, those who have sinned on earth and shall yet be saved, for by these medicines it is fitting that every soul be healed. And though a soul be healed, its wounds are seen before God, no longer as wounds but as trophies. So, on the other hand, as we have been punished here by sorrow and by penance, we will be rewarded in heaven by the courteous love of our Lord God almighty who desires that no one coming to him loses in any degree by all such labours. For he holds sin as a sorrow and pain to his lovers, in whom he assigns no blame for his love.

The reward we will receive will not be little, it will be high, glorious and full of praise. And so shall shame be turned to honour and with it joy; for it is the will of our courteous Lord that his servants should not despair of their grievous falling; for when we fall he is not hindered from still loving us.

Peace and love are ever in us, working in our very ground, yet we are not always in peace and love. He wants us to know and take heed: he is the ground of our whole life in love, and moreover he is our everlasting keeper and mightily he defends us against our enemies who come at us full fell and fierce. (Our need is all the greater the more we give them occasion by our falling.)

40

THE mark of sovereign friendship of our courteous Lord is that he keeps us so tenderly while we are in sin; and furthermore he touches us so secretly and shows us our sin by the sweet light of mercy and grace. But when we see ourselves so foul, then we fear that God is angry with us for our sins; and so we are stirred of the Holy Spirit by contrition to prayer and conceive the desire to reform our life with all our might in order to satisfy God's anger, and after a time we find rest in our soul and ease of conscience. Then we are hopeful that God has forgiven our sins, and so it is.

Then our courteous Lord shows himself to our soul, with merriment and glad cheer, with friendly welcoming, as if he himself had been in pain and prison, and sweetly he speaks these words:

'My darling, I am glad you are come to me. In all this woe I have ever been with you; now see at last my loving: how are we oned in bliss.'

In this way are sins forgiven by mercy and grace as our soul is received with honour and in joy, just as it will be when we come to heaven; whenever this happens it is by the grace and working of the Holy Spirit and the power of Christ's passion. Here I understood in full that everything is disposed towards us by the great goodness of God insomuch as, when at last we are at peace and charity within ourselves, we are truly saved. Yet since we may never enjoy this to the full as long as we are still here, therefore we must be content to live the while in patient prayer and lovely longing for our Lord Jesus. For he longs ceaselessly to bring us to fullest joy, as it has already been set down where he showed his spiritual thirst.

But now, should someone, learning of this same spiritual comfort, be foolish enough to say or even think: 'If this be true, then it is a good idea to sin in order to win more merit', or else to think any less of sin, beware that this is a temptation, for truly, if it should come, it is false and from the enemy. The same true love that touches us all by his blessed comfort, that same blessed love teaches us that we should hate sin and hold fast to love. And I am sure, in my heart, the more that all human souls see this in the courteous love of our Lord God, the more they will loathe sin, the greater their sense of shame. For if all the pains contained in hell, on earth and in purgatory – including death and all – were set before us, we ought rather to choose all that pain than sin itself; for sin is so vile and so greatly to be hated that it compares to no other pain save the very pain of sin itself. And I was shown no harder hell than sin, for of its very nature, the soul knows no other hell but sin. Yet fixing our intent in love and meekness we are made all fair and clean by the working of mercy and grace. For as mighty and as wise as God is to save us, so is he most willing; it is Christ himself who is the ground of all Christian law, and he taught us to do good as against evil.

In this we see that he himself is that love, for he does to us as he bids us do to others; for it is his will we be like him in perfecting endless love in ourselves and towards our fellow Christians. Inasmuch as his love is never broken towards us when we sin, so does he will that it is never broken within ourselves or towards our fellow Christians; rather we should hate the sin itself but endlessly love every soul as God loves it. Then shall we come to hate sin as God hates it, and love the soul as he does.

These words he said are lasting comfort: 'I keep you most surely.'

THE FOURTEENTH SHOWING

41

Julian begins to speak of prayer:
she is characteristically enabling and at once original and sure-footed.
'I am the ground of your beseeking ...
how should it be that you should not have whom you seek?'

AFTER this our Lord showed me about prayer. And in this showing, according to our Lord's meaning, I saw two conditions for prayer: one is rightfulness, the other sure trust.

For many times our trust is not complete; we are not sure

whether God hears us, or so it seems, owing to our unworthiness, and we feel quite empty. How often are we barren and dry at prayer, sometimes seeming even more so when they are done. Yet this is only in our feelings and caused by our own folly, coming from weakness; I have felt as much myself.[49]

And among all this confusion of thoughts, our Lord suddenly came to mind and showed me these words, saying:

'I am the ground of your beseeking:[50] first it is my will that you have it, and then I make you want it: now since I make you seek, and then you do seek, how should it then be that you should not have whom you seek?'

And in this first reason alone, that he is the ground, but then strengthened by the three that follow, our good Lord shows us mighty comfort, as may be seen in these very same words. For in the first reason he speaks thus: 'And then you do seek'; and here he shows the very great pleasure and reward without end that he wants to give us for all our seeking. And in the sixth reason, where he says, 'how should it then be …'and so on, this is to state the impossible: for it is utterly impossible that we should seek mercy and grace and not have it. Quite simply, all the things that our good Lord makes us seek and ask for, he has ordained as ours from without beginning. Here we see it is not our own seeking that is the cause of God's goodness: this he showed plainly in all his sweet words, especially when he said: 'I am the ground.' And our good Lord wants this to be known by his lovers on earth; for the more we recognize it, the more will we seek, as we properly understand the full wisdom of our Lord's meaning.

---

[49] This phrase is one of the rare moments when Julian appears to emerge from her anonymity; she cries out in sympathy with us as she tells how tough it is to pray regularly.

[50] *Beseke*: can mean pray or beg for, or to seek after, search for. Julian appears to embrace both meanings – similar to our modern 'seek '. Clearly prayer for Julian is far more than the prayer of petition – rather it is our seeking the Presence and Person of God: see later: 'beseeking is a new, lasting will of the soul … fastened into the will of our Lord …'

Beseeking is a new, lasting will of the soul, coming from grace, by which it is oned and fastened into the will of our Lord by the sweet, silent working of the Holy Spirit. For it is our Lord himself who is the first to receive our prayer, as I see it; he takes it most thankfully, and with great joy he sends it up above and sets it among his treasures where it will never perish. So that it is there before God with all his holy ones, being received continually so that it speeds our every need. And when at length we shall receive our bliss, it will be given back to us as part of our joy, with endless praise and thanks from him.

Our Lord is full of gladness and delight at our prayers; he looks out for them, for he wants them longingly. For by means of his grace they make us grow like himself in condition as we are in kind;[51] this is his blessed will for he says:

'Pray inwardly although you think it savours you not, for it is profitable even though you feel nothing; though you see nothing, and yes, though you think there is nothing you can do; for in dryness and barrenness, in sickness and in feebleness, all the while your prayers are most pleasing to me, although you think it savours you little or nothing. It is the same with all your living prayers in my sight.'

Because of the reward and the endless thanks he wants to give us, he eagerly desires to have us pray continually in his sight. God accepts the good will and hard efforts of his servant, however we feel. Because of this, he is pleased when we work at our prayers and in good living with his help and grace, fixing our gaze quietly on him until that time when we have him whom we seek in the fullness of joy, that is, Jesus. This was

---

[51] condition: in ME can denote a) situation, circumstance; b) mode of being; c) personal disposition. Here Julian would appear to embrace all three, since she is talking not just about what happens in time through mercy and grace but our ultimate bliss. In our kind (i.e. nature, meaning substance+sensuality) we are made in the image of God, but 'in our sensuality we are failing ... which God will restore by mercy and grace' (ch. 57). Thus condition is our kind 'on the mend' through his working of mercy and grace, and we join in this 'working' by our beseeking.

shown before in the fifteenth showing, in these words: 'You shall have me as your reward.'

As well as seeking, thanking also belongs to prayer. Thanking is a new, inner familiarity with him, full of reverence and loving fear as with all our might we bring ourself to join the work our good Lord is stirring within us, inwardly enjoying and thanking him. Sometimes this simply overflows, and we break our silence crying: 'Good Lord, give me mercy; blessed may you be!' And other times, the heart is dry and lacks all feeling, or else there may be a temptation from our enemy: then by good sense and by grace we are driven to cry out aloud again to our Lord, recalling his blessed passion and his great goodness. And the virtue of our Lord's word turns into[52] the soul, lifting the heart so that by his grace it enters into its true work; and so, gently enabled, it prays with true enjoyment in our Lord; then is there full blissful thanking in his sight.

42

Julian's approach to prayer reveals her own assimilation of the teachings behind her showings: in particular, how we are to approach God in prayer when we know we are sinners.
As always, our starting point is God rather than self:
'I am the ground.'

OUR Lord wishes that we understand well three things that belong to our praying. The first is by whom and how our prayer arises. By whom he shows when he says: 'I am the ground'; and how is by his goodness alone, inasmuch as he tells us: 'First it is my will.'

---

52 Wordknot: 'turns or comes into' and 'turns (it) into'. The soul is transformed.

And the second is the manner of our praying and its pur- pose; this is simply that our will be turned into the will of our Lord, with continual joy. This he means when he says: 'I make you seek me.' As for the third, that we know the fruit and end of our praying, this is none other than we be oned and like to our Lord in all things. And with this meaning and for this end all this lovely lesson was shown; he will help us achieve it and we will make it happen just as he himself has said, blessed may he be!

This is our Lord's will, that both our praying and our trust be equally generous; for if in praying our trust is not great, and we fail to do full honour to our Lord, then we waste time and do ourselves harm. I believe the cause is that we do not truly grasp that our Lord is the ground from which all our praying springs, and we ignore that it is given us by the grace of his love. For if we knew this, it would enable us to trust that we might have, of our Lord's gift, all we desire; of this I am sure, that no one sincerely asks for mercy and grace without mercy and grace first being given.

Yet sometimes we are mindful that we have prayed a long time and still we feel that we have not received what we asked for; but all the same, we must not be put down; for I am sure of our Lord's meaning in this, that either we must wait for a better time, or an increase in grace, or perhaps an even greater gift. He desires us to know truly that he alone is full Being; and he wishes that our understanding be grounded in this knowing, with all our might and all our intent and all our meaning; and he wants us to take this ground as our standing-place and as our freehold.[53] And by the gracious light of himself he wants us to understand the following things. The first is our noble and excellent making; the second, our precious and dearworthy

---

53 Our stede and our wonying: stede, as in homestead, means our standing-place, where we find ourself; wonying is dwelling or home. The combination of the two suggests somewhere that is both home and permanent, our soul's free- hold – and that this is in the very ground of God.

again-buying;[54] the third is that he has made all things beneath us to serve us and how, for our love, he keeps them.

His purpose in all this is as if he were to say: 'Behold and see, I have done all this before you even pray, and now you are, and here you are praying to me.' By this he means that we should know full well that the greatest deeds are already accomplished, as holy Church teaches us. As we behold this with thankfulness, we ought to pray for the deed that is being done here and now: namely that he may rule us and guide us in this life and so bring us to his bliss. To this single end he has done all. And this is his meaning: seeing what he is doing, we should pray for it to come about. Just to pray in itself is not enough; for if we simply pray without seeing what he is doing, this makes us heavy-hearted and full of doubt, which is not to his service. Equally, if we see what he does yet do not pray, we fail to discharge our debt to him. May it never be so, or rather one must say, it could never be so in his sight. But to see his purpose, to recognize what he is doing, and to pray for that end, this gives him great praise and then we too make great strides.

So it is with all things that our Lord has planned, he wants us to pray that they come to fruition, whether in particular or in a more general way. Then the joy and happiness that is his, the thanks and honour that shall be ours, because of it, are beyond the understanding of mortal creatures. This is how I see it.

For prayer is a right understanding of the fullness of joy that is to come, as well as longing and the sure trust that it will be ours. Failing to have the full joy that has been promised us makes us long for it all the more; but true understanding and love, mindful of our sweet Saviour's purpose, brings with it the grace to trust in him. And in these two workings – of longing and of trust – our Lord beholds us continually; such is our dutiful task, and in his goodness he expects nothing less of us.

---

54 This literal Englishing of the Latin word *redemption* was much used in Julian's time, not least by the reformer Wycliff.

Therefore it is up to us to work diligently, and when we have done all we should do, to count it as nothing, for that is the truth. We should do as best we may, counting truly on his mercy and grace, and all that fails us we shall find in him.

And this is what he means where he says: 'I am the ground of all your seeking.' And in this blissful word that came with the showing I knew we would overcome all our weakness, all our doubtful dreads.

43

Her definition of prayer is very simple:
'Prayer witnesses to the soul's will being like to God's will.'
Moreover, it is prompted, enabled and enacted by God's grace:
'Whenever we see our need of prayer, then our good Lord follows us,
to help our desire ... his marvellous and generous goodness
fulfilling all our powers.'

PRAYER makes the soul one with God; for even though the soul is always alike to God in its nature and substance since it is restored by grace, yet often it is unlike him for the sin on our part. So that prayer witnesses to the soul's will being like to God's will; then is our conscience healed as we are enabled by grace. This is how he teaches us to pray, firmly trusting that we shall have it; for he holds us in love and wants us to partner him in his good deed. Therefore he stirs us in prayer to do what most pleases him. And because of these prayers and our good will that results, his own gift, he will reward us with endless merit. This was shown in the words: 'And then you do seek ...' In this saying, God showed such great pleasure and so much liking, as though he were utterly beholden to us for every good deed of ours – yet it is always he that does them. So it is when we pray sincerely to do all things that are pleasing to him. It is as if he said: 'What could please me more than when you pray mightily, wisely and with good will for all that I will do?' So it is by this prayer the soul comes to accord with God.

But when our courteous Lord shows himself by grace to our soul, we have all our desire; in that time we see fit to leave aside prayer as all our attention, all our might is set wholly on beholding him. But this is a high and unknowable prayer, as I see it. For now our reasons for praying come together in the sight and contemplation of him to whom we pray, marvellously enjoying him with reverent dread and such great sweetness and delight that our prayer is nothing any more: instead it is he that stirs within us.

And I know very well that the more the soul sees of God, the more it desires him by his grace. But when we see him no longer, then we feel the need and cause to pray – its very failing enables us to find our Jesus. For when the soul is set about and troubled and left alone in restlessness, then is the time to pray so as to make oneself supple and buxom* to God.⁵⁵ As to himself, no manner of prayer may make God supple to us since his love is ever alike in our regard.

And so I saw that whenever we see our need of prayer, then our good Lord follows us, to help our desire. Or when, by special grace, we behold him plainly, seeing need of none but him, then we follow him as he draws us to himself in love. For I both saw and felt his marvellous and generous goodness fulfilling all our powers; then I saw that his continual working in every conceivable thing is done so goodly, so wisely and so mightily that it defies imagination and all that we can guess or think. Then we can do no more than gaze on him with single, overwhelming desire to be all one with him, settled in his dwelling, enjoying his love, delighting in his goodness. And then shall we, by his sweet grace, with continuing and meek

---

55 buxum to God: Julian would have used this word because it meant just as she intended: OED has: meek, gracious, obliging.

prayer come to him in this life by many secret touchings of sweet inner sights and feelings in the measure that our simple souls can bear it; and this is wrought, and shall be, by the grace of the Holy Spirit, until we shall come to die in longing for love. Then shall we all come into our Lord, then we ourselves will know clearly and God will have us fully. We will be hidden in God without end, seeing him truly, feeling him fully, hearing him in spirit and smelling him delectably and swallowing him sweetly: then will we see God face to face, homely and fully; the creature that is made shall see and behold God who is maker without end; for none may see God thus and live afterwards, that is to say in this mortal life. But when he of his special grace shows himself here, he strengthens a creature above itself, measuring that showing according to his own will, and as is profitable in that time.

44

Christian mystics have always seen the connection between the Trinity
and the human soul. Not only are we made in his image and likeness, but
the workings of our redemption, the way we walk in and
towards God is trinitarian.
Julian describes her experience of this simply and powerfully.

TIME and again God showed in all these revelations that we work his will always and do him honour continually without stint. And the nature of this work was shown in the first revelation in marvellous ground, for it was shown in the working of the soul of our blissful Lady St Mary, in all her truth and wisdom. And I hope, by the grace of God, to tell it just as I saw.

Truth sees God, and wisdom beholds God, and of these two comes the third: that is a holy marvellous delight in God, which is love. For where truth and wisdom truly are, there too is love flowing from them both, and all is of God's making; for he is the endless sovereign truth, endless sovereign wisdom, endless sovereign love – unmade. And the soul is a creature in[56] God, that has the same properties though they be made. And so now and evermore it does what it was made for: it sees God, it beholds God and it loves God. And because of this, God takes enjoyment in his creature, and the creature in God, both endlessly marvelling. In which marvelling we see our God, our Lord, our Maker, so high, so great and so good compared to that which is made, so that of ourselves we seem nothing. But the brightness and the clearness of truth and wisdom makes us see and know that we are made for love: in which love God endlessly keeps us.

45

Returning to her continuing difficulty about sin and mindful of the Church's teaching, Julian continues to question and to seek.

GOD judges us by our human nature which he keeps forever one with him, where it is whole and safe without end; and this judgement stems from his rightfulness. By contrast, before human beings we are judged by our changing sensuality* which seems now one thing, now another, according to which part it takes after and how it shows outwardly. And so this judgement is wayward; for sometimes it is good and tolerant, and another time it is hard and grievous. And inasmuch as it is good and tolerant, then it touches on God's

---

[56] 'In' means 'of': That is, 'creature of God'. Yet to retain 'in' stresses the indwelling of the Father as maker, a characteristically Julian insight.

rightfulness; yet when it is hard and grievous, our good Lord Jesus reforms it by his mercy and grace through the merit of his blessed passion, and so is it brought into his rightfulness. And in this way these two shall be brought together as one, yet they shall both be known separately in heaven without end.

The first judgement comes from God's rightfulness, that is, of his high endless love; and this is that fair and gentle judgement that was shown in all this lovely revelation where I saw that he assigned no manner of blame to us. And, though this was sweet and delightful to behold, I could not fully rest at ease; and this was due to the Church's own judgement that I understood before, which was still continually in my sight. According to this judgement, I must confess myself a sinner; and equally by the same judgement I knew that sinners must at some time deserve blame and wrath. Yet I could see neither of these two in God, so my longing to understand was more than I can tell. For the higher judgement was shown me by God himself and I must needs accept it; yet the lower was taught me by holy Church, therefore I might in no way leave aside this lower judgement.

This then was my desire, that I might see in God in what manner the judgement taught here by holy Church is true in his sight, and in what way I was meant to understand it. Then both truths would stand: God would be rightly honoured and, for myself, I would know the right path. To all this, I had no other answer but a marvellous example of a lord and a servant, as I shall tell afterwards, where it was powerfully shown. And yet I still desire, and will do till my life's end, to be given grace to know these two judgements as they apply to me. For all heavenly things, and all earthly things that belong to heaven, are understood in these two judgements. And the more understanding, by the grace and enlightenment of the Holy Spirit, that we have of these two judgements, the more clearly will we come to see and know our failings. And the more we see them, the more naturally by grace will we long to be filled full of endless joy and bliss. We are made for this, for already our human

nature is held in God's bliss, as indeed it has been since it was
first made, and so shall it be without end.

46

'His charity and his unity suffers him not to be wroth ...
it is against the property of might to be angry.
For our soul is fully oned to God of his own goodness
so that between the soul and God there may be right nought.'

HERE in our passing life we live in our sensuality so that
we may never know our true self, except in faith; when
we come to know and see truly, then we shall truly see
and clearly know our Lord God in fullness of joy. And therefore it must be true that the nearer we be to our bliss, the more
we shall long for him, both by nature and by grace.[57] We can
have some knowledge of ourself in this life by seeking the continual help and virtue of our higher nature. And we can increase
and grow in this knowledge by the furthering and quickening
of mercy and grace; but we may never fully know ourselves
until our last moment, that point when this passing life with all
its accompanying pain and woe will come to an end. Therefore
it belongs to us, both by nature and by grace, to desire and
long with all our might to know ourselves in the fullness of
everlasting joy.

And yet in all this time, from the beginning to the end of it,

---

[57] A keynote in Julian's theology and mystical map is the idea of human
nature working out its path to God in grace. Human kind (our nature) is
made and held in the Father; before time, it is taken by the Son: in the act
of his becoming man and the deeds of his again-making, or redemption, he
gives us his virtue or power in love – that is grace, the working of the Holy
Spirit. Our simple task – to which Julian continually exhorts us – is to collaborate in this working.

I had two kinds of beholding. One was the endless and continual love with sureness of keeping and blissful salvation, which is the whole meaning of this revelation; and the other was the common teaching of holy Church in which from birth I was informed and grounded, and which I have always tried to use and better understand. And my awareness of this never left me; and indeed, in the showing I was never stirred or led away from the Church's teaching on any single point. On the contrary, I was taught in this to love and cherish it, for by this means I could, by the help of our Lord and his grace, have increase and be raised to more heavenly knowledge and a higher loving.

And thus in all this beholding I thought I needed to see and know that we are sinners who do many evil things that we ought to avoid, and leave many good deeds undone that we ought to do.[58] So that we deserve both pain and wrath.

And notwithstanding all this, I saw quite plainly that our Lord was never wroth nor ever shall be, for he is God: he is good, he is life, he is truth, he is love, he is peace; while his charity and his unity suffers him not to be wroth. Indeed, I saw truly that it is against the property of might to be angry, against the property of his wisdom and against the property of his goodness. Our soul is oned to him, who is unchangeable goodness, and between God and our soul there is neither wrath nor need of forgiveness in his sight. For our soul is fully oned to God of his own goodness, so that between the soul and God there may be right nought.

The soul was led by love to this understanding and drawn by might in every revelation; our good Lord showed it to be thus, and how it is so is truly of his great goodness. And it is his will that we desire to learn, that is to say, inasmuch as it is proper for a creature to know it. For everything that this

---

[58] The Sarum confession used these words, which are nowadays still familiar in the Anglican rite, although the form disappeared from the Roman mass with the reforms of Trent. It still survives, however, in the Carthusian ritual.

simple soul came to understand, God wills it to be shown and known. And the things that he will hold secret, he himself hides them mightily and wisely, for love. And I saw in the same showing that many things are hidden away in secret which may never become known until such time as God of his goodness has made us worthy of seeing them.

And with this I am well content, abiding in our Lord's will on this high marvel. And for now, I yield myself to my mother holy Church, as any simple child should.

47

Julian continues her quest:
she has learnt that God does not blame us for sin
(she could see no wrath in God),
yet she knows full well the pain of sin as it takes us from God
(as we 'fall into ourselves').
She is to find answer presently in the 'marvellous parable
of the lord and servant'.

OUR soul has a debt on twin counts: one is that we must reverently marvel;[59] the other is that we meekly suffer, always finding our joy in God. For he wants us to know that within a short time, we will see clearly in him all that we desire. Notwithstanding all this, I beheld and wondered greatly about God's mercy and forgiveness. For according to the teaching I had before, I understood that the mercy of God should mean the forgiveness of his wrath, after we had sinned. As it seemed to me, to the soul whose intention and desire is to love, the wrath of God was harder than any other pain; and

---

[59] Julian is recognizing here that every Christian has a duty to pray, daily contemplating God's workings in reverence.

therefore I took it that the forgiveness of his wrath should be one of the principal points of his mercy. But for all I could behold and desire to learn, I could not see this point in any of the showings. Yet of how I understood and came to see the workings of mercy, I shall say something, as much as God will give me grace.

I understood that we are changeable in this life: overcome by frailty we fall into sin. We lose all our strength, all common sense – also our will is overlaid; in these moments, we feel nothing but tempest, sorrow and woe. And the cause of all this is blindness: we cannot see God. For if we were to see God continually, then there would be none of this mischief, nor any manner of stirring that yearning to enslave us in sin.

This was what I saw, how I felt at this time; and I thought that the sight and the feeling was high and plenteous and gracious compared to those common feelings we have in our day-to-day life; yet I thought it was small and low compared to the great desire that the soul has to see God. And I felt in me five kinds of working which are these: enjoying, mourning, desire, dread and sure hope.

Enjoying, in that God gave me to understand and know that it was himself I saw. Mourning, that is in failing. Desire, that I might see him ever more and more, understanding and knowing that we shall never have full rest until we see him truly and clearly in heaven. Dread came all the while, as it seemed to me the sight might fail and I would be left to myself. Sure hope was in that endless love in which I saw I should be kept by his mercy and brought unto his bliss. And the joy in his sight with sure hope that his mercy was keeping me brought such feeling of comfort that any mourning or dread seemed no great pain to bear.

In spite of all this, I knew in this showing of God that such a way of seeing him cannot be continuous in this life, by reason of his own dignity and so that our endless joy may grow. And therefore we often fail in his sight, and presently we fall into ourselves. Then we find we have no more feeling of right, nothing but contrariness within ourself, that is the old root of our first sin with all that stems from our own contrivances; in this way we are troubled and tempest-tossed, with feeling of sins and of many varied pains, in spirit and body. As we know only too well in this life of ours.[60]

48

BUT our good Lord the Holy Spirit, who is endless life, dwells in our soul. It is he who keeps us full surely, for there he works a peace that brings us to ease by grace, attuning us to God so that we become his docile[61] listeners. And this is the way of mercy upon which our Lord leads us continually for as long as we are here in this changing life;[62] for I saw no wrath except on our own part; and this he forgives in us.

Such wrath is none other than our fractiousness and contrariness to peace and love; which comes either of failing of might or failing of wisdom or failing of goodness, which failing is not in God, but comes from our part.[63] For by sin and wretchedness we have in us a wretched and continual contrariness to peace and love; and this he showed me often in his lovely look of ruth and pity. For the ground of mercy is love,

---

[60] Julian, the great optimist, hits her lowest point here as she beholds our human predicament, blind and apparently removed from God.

[61] Again Julian's word is buxum.

[62] A clear reference to a path of spirituality that has become well developed in the Eastern Church, that of the pneumatikos, the one who listens to the Holy Spirit within.

[63] 'We fall into ourselves' (cf. ch. 47): Julian's existential definition of our sinning. And when we fall into ourselves, we leave aside the working of the Trinity – 'might, wisdom, goodness'.

and the working of mercy is our being kept in love; this was shown in such manner that I could not understand the property of mercy except as it were love alone. (I may only tell how it seemed to me.) Mercy is a sweet and gracious working, in love, mingled with plenteous pity. For mercy works in keeping us. Mercy works by turning all things to good. Mercy, for love, suffers us to fail by measure and design.[64] And inasmuch as we fail, so much we die; and die we must, since we fail in sight and feeling of God, who is our only life.

Our failing is dreadful, our falling is shameful, our dying is sorrowful; but in all this, the sweet eye of pity and love never looks away from us, neither does the working of mercy cease. For I beheld the property of mercy, and I beheld the property of grace. And these have two ways of working in one same love.

Now mercy has the property of pity, for it belongs to the Motherhood[65] in tender love; and grace is an honourable property which belongs to the royal Lordship in the same love. Mercy works by keeping, suffering, quickening and healing, all from tenderness of love. Grace works by raising up, rewarding and endlessly surpassing whatever our love and labour might deserve, spreading abroad and proclaiming the high, plentiful largesse of God's royal Lordship in his marvellous courtesy. All this comes from the abundance of his love. For grace works our dreadful failing into plenteous endless solace, and grace works our shameful falling into high, honourable rising, and grace works our sorrowful dying into holy and blissful life. For I saw full surely that whenever our contrariness causes us pain, shame and sorrow here on earth, without fail grace works for us solace, honour and bliss in heaven. So much will this abound, that when we come up and receive the sweet reward which

---

[64] 'by measure' is the scriptural sense found in Job and Wisdom: God's set plan for ruling and guiding all things to their end is Wisdom beyond our understanding.

[65] The first reference to God's Motherhood which Julian later develops and appropriates to Christ.

grace has worked on our behalf, we shall thank and bless our Lord, endlessly grateful that we ever suffered so.

And this property of blessed love we shall know in God, which we might never have known had not woe gone before. And once I had seen all this, I knew that I must grant that the mercy of God and his forgiveness is to slake and waste our wrath.

49

Julian returns to her conviction that there is no wrath in God:
'If God could be wroth even for a touch, then we should have no more life.'

THIS was a high wonder to the soul which was shown continually in all the revelations and beheld with great diligence: that our Lord God, of his very nature, may not forgive since he may never be angry – for that would be impossible. This is what was shown: our whole life is grounded and rooted in love, for without love we may not live. And therefore once the soul, by God's special grace, sees to such a degree the high wonder of the goodness of God that we are oned to him in love without end, it is utterly impossible that God should be wroth. For wrath and friendship are two opposites. He who wastes and destroys our wrath, making us meek and mild, must accordingly be ever in the same love, meek and mild, which is contrary to wrath. For I saw very clearly that where our Lord appears, there peace is established so that wrath has no more place. And I saw no manner of wrath in God, neither for short nor long time, for in truth, as I understood, if God could be wroth even for a touch, then we should have no more life, nor standing-place, nor being. For as truly as we have our being from the endless might of God, from his endless wisdom and from his endless goodness, so too we have our keeping from the endless might of God, from his endless wisdom, from his endless goodness. Though we feel within ourself discord, wretchedness and strife, yet are we all mercifully enclosed in the mildness of God and in his meekness, in his kindness and his openness.[66] For I saw full surely that all our endless friendship, our home, our life and our being is in God; for the same endless goodness that keeps us when we sin and saves us from perishing, the same endless goodness continually coaxes[67] us towards peace away from our wrath and contrary failing, and makes us see our need with true dread, so that we seek our God for his forgiveness as grace makes us long for our salvation.

It is this wrath and contrariness within us that brings us tribulation, unease and woe due to our blindness and frailty, yet we are sure and safe so that, by the merciful keeping of God, we will not perish.

Yet we will never be fully safe and know our endless joy till we be finally in peace and love; that is to say, fully pleased with God and with all his works and all his judgements, loving and at peace within ourself and with our fellow Christians and with all them that love God, as befits love. This is worked in us by God's goodness. Thus I saw that God is our very peace, and he is our sure keeper when we are at peace within ourself, and he works continually to bring us into his endless peace. And so when we are made meek and mild by the working of mercy and grace, we are fully safe. Then suddenly the soul is oned to God when it is truly at peace in itself, for in him no wrath is to be found. And thus I saw that when we are all in peace and in love we find no contrariness, and no means for that contrariness to act within us.

---

[66] Buxumhede: buxomness. Julian has already used the word (ch. 43 and elsewhere) in our relating to God, being open to him, making ourself gracious, obliging; now here she applies it to God's attitude towards us, another variant of his courtesy.

[67] Tretyth: treats, parleys, negotiates: the inner dialogue between God and the soul.

Rather, our Lord in his goodness makes it work to help us; for such contrariness is cause of all our troubles and all our woe, yet our Lord Jesus takes them and sends them up to heaven where they are made more sweet and delectable than heart may think or tongue may tell;[68] and when we come there we shall find them waiting, all changed into very fine and everlasting rewards. So it is that God is our steadfast home, and he shall be our full happiness and make us unchanging as he is, once we are there.

50

IN this mortal life, mercy and forgiveness is the path that leads us steadily to grace. And because of the tempest and sorrow that fall across our way, we are often dead, according to humankind's judgement on earth; yet in the sight of God, the soul that shall be saved was never dead nor will it be. Yet I wondered and would ponder with all the diligence in my power, thinking to myself: 'Good Lord, I see that you are very truth, and I well know that we sin grievously every day and are much to be blamed; and I can never avoid this truth, yet on your part, I can see no suggestion of blame. How may this be so?' For I knew from the common teaching of holy Church, as well as from my own experience, how the guilt of our sin continually hangs upon us, from the very first human being until such time we ourselves arrive in heaven. This then was my difficulty, that I saw our Lord God displays no more blame towards us than if we were as clean and as holy as his angels in heaven. My mind was confused by these two contradictions;

---

68 Julian refers to the Jubilus of St Bernard, *Jesu dulcis memoria*, 'Jesus, the very thought of thee,' which she would have known as a popular hymn and prayed privately in its Latin version.

I was most anxious to see clearly, yet could find no rest for fear that I might lose sight of his blessed presence, leaving me still ignorant of how he truly beholds us in our sin. For either I needed to see in God that sin was all done away with, or else I needed to see in God how he himself sees it, and thereby I might come to know how I ought view sin and the manner in which we are blamed.

This longing lasted all the while I was beholding him and yet I was still impatient with great fear and perplexity, thinking all the while: 'If I were to take it this way, that we are not sinners neither are we to blame, it seems as though I should err and fail to find the truth. And yet if it is true that we are indeed sinners and to blame for it, good Lord, how is it that I cannot see this truth in you, who are my God and Maker, in whom I desire to see all truths?'

Three motives I see that make me bold to ask: the first is that it is such a small thing, for if it were some high truth, I would be fearful; the second is that it is so common, for again if it were special and secret, I would equally be full of fear; and third, I really need to know it, or so it seems to me, simply so that in my living here I may know the difference between good and evil; then by reason and grace I may distinguish them and come to love good and hate evil, right as holy Church teaches.

I cried inwardly with all my might, seeking God's help, begging him thus: 'Ah! Lord Jesus, King of bliss, how shall I ever be saved? Who is there to teach me and tell me what I need to know, if all the while I may not see it in you?'

51

There follows the parable of the servant,
the response to her compelling quest about the nature of sin.
After twenty years, Julian begins to glimpse its full meaning:
Christ now stands for Adam, the first servant;
to do his Father's bidding, he falls into the Maiden's womb
and into hell — then in power he restores us to his glory with his Father.

AND then our courteous Lord answered by showing full mistily a wonderful example of a lord who has a servant; and he enlightened my understanding as to them both. This sight was shown doubly in regard of the lord; and it was shown doubly in regard of the servant. The first part was shown spiritually with bodily likeness, and the other was shown more spiritually without any image.

As for the first part, this is how I saw it: I was shown two persons in bodily likeness, namely a lord and a servant; and at the same time God gave me spiritual understanding. The lord sits solemnly in rest and in peace, while the servant stands by, reverently before his lord, ready to do his lord's will. The lord looks upon his servant with very sweet and loving gaze, and then meekly he sends him to a certain place to do his will. The servant not only goes, but he starts out suddenly and runs with great haste for the love he has to do his lord's will. And straightway he falls into a boggy dell and takes very great hurt. And then he groans and moans and wails and writhes, but neither can he rise up nor may he help himself in any way. And in of all this, the most mischief that I saw for him was his lack of comfort; for he could not turn his face and look towards his loving lord, who, still very close to him, was his only comfort. But like a man for the time being disabled and out of his wits, all he had feeling for was his own pain and the woes he suffered.

In that woe were seven great pains. The first was the sore

bruising that he had taken as he fell, which was great pain to him. The second was the heaviness in his body. The third was feebleness following these two. The fourth, that he was blinded in his reason and stunned in his mind such that he almost forgot his great love. The fifth was he could not rise. The sixth was the most remarkable to me, that he lay alone; I looked all about and searched both far and near, high and low, and I could see no one that might help him. The seventh, the place he lay in was throughout its length both hard and grievous. I wondered how this servant might suffer all this woe so meekly. Then I looked close at him to see if I could perceive any fault, or if perhaps the lord would find any blame in him; but truly there was none to see. For it was only his own good will and great willingness that had caused his falling; and he was as keen and as inwardly well disposed as when he stood before his lord all ready to do his will. And even so his good lord continued to behold him with the same love and tenderness. Yet now it was a twofold gaze; outwardly, his look was most meek and mild, having great ruth and pity: such was the first. Another, more inward and spiritual, was shown me. By leading my understanding into the lord, I saw that he was greatly pleased on account of the glorious and noble rest that he wills and shall bring his servant to by his plentiful grace. Such was the second showing; and now once more my understanding was led back to the first, while still keeping both in mind.

Then the courteous lord spoke his mind: 'Lo, lo, my beloved servant. What harm and disease he has taken in the service he undertook for my love, yes, and with such good will! Is it not right that I reward him for his terror and his fright, his hurt and his wounds and all his woe? And not only this, does it not fall to me to give him a gift that would be better and more reward to him than ever he had before? Or else it seems I give him no thanks at all.' And at this, a spiritual showing of the lord's meaning flooded my soul, in which I saw that it simply had to be, given his own great goodness and his understanding his honour, that this most dear servant whom he so loved should be rewarded truly and blissfully without end more than ever he had been before his fall. Yes, and to such a degree that his falling and all the woe he thereby suffered should become a high, surmounting honour and his endless bliss.

And at this point, the showing of this parable vanished, and our good Lord led forward my understanding into the sight of the revelation and the way it was shown, to the very end. But notwithstanding his guidance, my fascination at the parable never left me. I was sure that it was given in answer to my desire, yet at that time I could not grasp its meaning fully enough to satisfy me.

For in the servant that was shown for Adam, as I will say, were many different properties that simply could not all belong solely to Adam on his own. And so, at this time, I was very confused; and the full understanding of this marvellous parable was not given to me then. There were in particular three properties of the revelation which still remained mysterious. Notwithstanding, I saw and understood that every revelation contains much that is still hidden, yet I ought to detail these three properties, for in them I could discern some meaning.

The first is the beginning of teaching that I understood therein at the time. The second is the inner knowledge I have gained since then. And the third is the whole revelation from beginning to its end, that is to say, this book itself, which our Lord God in his goodness often brings easily to the eyes of my understanding. And these three are so joined, as I understand it, that I cannot, nor may I, separate them. And by this three-as-one teaching I have the means whereby I ought to believe and trust in our Lord God that of the same goodness by which he showed it, and for the same end, right so of the same goodness and for the same end, he will declare it to us when it is his will.

For, twenty years less three months after the time of the showing, I had teaching inwardly, as I shall tell: 'It is your task to take heed of all the properties and conditions that were shown in the parable, though you think they are mysterious and hard to see.' I assented willingly and with great desire; I examined inwardly and with care all the points and properties that were shown me at the time, as much as my wit and understanding would allow. Beginning with my beholding the lord and his servant, the manner in which the lord sat, and the place where he sat, the colour of his clothing and the shape, his outward appearance and his inner goodness and his attractiveness.

The lord sat solemnly at rest and at peace; and so I understood that he is God. The servant that stood before the lord, I understood that he was showed for Adam, that is to say one man alone was shown at that time, and his falling, to make us understand thereby how God beholds anyone and his or her falling. For in the sight of God all men and women are as one person: that one person is all women, all men.[69] This man was hurt in his might and made full feeble; and he was stunned in his understanding, for he was turned away from beholding his lord. But his will was kept whole in God's sight; for I saw that our lord praised and approved his will, but in himself he was prevented and blinded from knowing this his true will; which was to him a great sorrow, a dire discomfort. For neither did he clearly see his loving lord, who is full meek and mild towards him, nor might he truly see how he himself is in the sight of his loving lord. And I know full well, when these two may be seen seen wisely and truly, we shall get rest and peace here, at least in part, and by his plentiful grace know its fulfilment in the bliss of heaven.

---

[69] for in the *syte* of God *al* man is *on* man *and* on man is *all* man: clumsy as the above inclusive rendering may read, it points up the meaning that Adam is the cipher of our one salvation. We fall together in Adam, the first man: we are raised together one in Christ, the second Adam.

Julian's basic problem remains unanswered:
if God does everything, how can sin be condoned?
Now she realizes that her answer lies hidden in this strange parable.
She must attend patiently.

And so began the teaching which I had at that time, by means of which I might come to know how he beholds us in our sin. And while I could see only pains, blame and punishment, yet our courteous Lord comforts and sorrows with us, looking always gladly upon the soul, loving us and longing all the while to bring us to his bliss.

The place where our lord sat was simple; he sat upon the barren earth, in a desert, alone in a wilderness. his clothing was wide and flowing, very seemly as befits a lord; the colour of his clothing was blue as azure, most solemn and fair. His mien was merciful, his face was bronzed, of feature fair; his eyes were dark and lustrous and showed a loving pity: his watchful gaze extended far and wide, seeming to fill the endless heavens. And with this lovely look he watched his servant continually, especially as he saw his falling; I thought to myself it might melt our hearts for love and break them in two for joy. This kindly looking showed a beautiful intermingling that was marvellous to behold: on one part it was compassion and pity, for the other joy and bliss. This joy and bliss so far surpasses the compassion and pity as heaven is above earth. For the pity was earthly and the bliss was of heaven. The compassion in the pity of the Father was for the falling of Adam, who is his most loved creature: the joy and the bliss belonged to his beloved Son who is always with the Father. His loving and merciful gaze filled the whole earth, even descending down to hell with Adam, and by this continual pity Adam was kept from everlasting death. And this same mercy and pity dwells with humankind until such time as we come up into heaven. But in this life we are blinded, and therefore we may not see the Father, our God, as he is. And whenever of his goodness he wishes to show himself to us, he does so familiarly, as man. Notwithstanding, I saw very clearly we should learn and come to know that the Father is not man. But his sitting on the barren earth in that desert has this meaning: he made the human soul to be his city, his own dwelling place, for it is to him the most pleasing of all his works. But since the time that Adam fell into sorrow and pain, he was not fit to serve that noble office; and yet our kind Father would prepare no other place, but he sits upon the earth abiding with mankind that is earthbound, until such time as his beloved Son by his grace has bought again his city into noble fairness by his hard travail.

The blueness of his clothing signified his steadfastness. The brown of his fair face, the winsome darkness of the eyes, spoke only of his holy purpose. The generosity of his clothing, that was shining fair, was a sign that he encompassed within himself all heavens, all joy, all bliss. And this was shown in an instant where I say 'my understanding was led into the lord', in which I saw him greatly enjoying the worshipful restoring he intends for his servant and shall bring him to by his plentiful grace.

Thus far, the parable only speaks to creation and Adam restored:
but why did God create in the first place, if he was complete unto himself?

And yet I marvelled as I continued to behold the lord and this same servant in more detail. For I saw the lord sitting solemnly and the servant standing reverently before his lord. And in the servant there is a double understanding: one without, another within. Outwardly he was simply clad, like a labourer ready for work; and he stood very near his lord, though not directly in front but rather to one side, on the left. His clothing was a white smock, unpleated, old and fast-stained with the sweat of his body; strait it fitted him, falling short about a handspan below the knee, threadbare too, seeming that soon it would be quite worn through, and ready to be ragged and rent. And at this I marvelled greatly, thinking to myself: 'Surely this is not the sort of clothing for a servant who is so loved to wear as he stands before his great lord.' And I saw inwardly, within him, a ground of love, such a love he bore towards the lord that was even like the love his lord bore towards him. The servant, in his wisdom, saw inwardly that there was only one thing to be done that would prove honourable service for his lord. Then the servant, of his love, not for his own reward nor of any gain to himself, started off in haste and ran at the bidding of his lord to perform the one task which was his will and worship. Outwardly, it seemed as if he had been a labourer continuously over a long time; yet by the inward sight I had, both of the lord and his servant, it seemed he was fresh, that is to say, newly begun to work, a servant never before sent out.

Now there was a treasure in the earth which the lord loved. I marvelled and thought what it could be. And I was answered in my understanding: 'It is a meat most desirable that will please the lord.' For I saw the lord sitting like a man, and I saw neither meat nor drink that one might serve him; that was one strangeness. Another was that this same solemn lord had no other servant than the one he had sent out. I considered this carefully, thinking what kind of labour it might be that the servant would do. And then I understood that he would do the greatest labour and the hardest work that is – he would be a gardener, delving and diking, toiling and sweating to turn the earth over and trench it; and he would water the plants in their time. And he would continue in all this work and make sweet water flow and noble fruits aplenty to spring forth; and these he would bring before his lord and serve them to him to please him. And he would never return again until he had prepared this meat all ready, just as he knew was to his lord's liking. And then he would take this meat, and drink too, together with the meat, and lay it worshipfully before his lord.

And all this time, the lord would be sitting in the same place awaiting his servant whom he had sent out. And still I wondered from where the servant came; for I saw in the lord that he had within himself endless life and all manner of goodness, save only that treasure that was in the earth – yet this itself was grounded in the lord in a marvellous deep vein of endless love

– but it was not completely acceptable until this same servant had prepared it so nobly and set it all before him, presenting it of his own accord. Apart from the lord there was nothing all around but wilderness; and so I could not understand at all what this example might mean, and still I continued to puzzle whence the servant had come.

Julian begins to recognize the beauty and meaning of her parable:
it sums up the whole story of our commerce with the Trinity.

Now in the servant is comprehended the Second Person of the Trinity; and in the servant is comprehended Adam, that is to say, all humankind. And therefore when I say 'the Son', it means the Godhead which is equal with the Father, and when I say 'the servant', it means Christ's manhood which is the true Adam. By the nearness of the servant the Son is understood, and by the standing to the left side is understood Adam. The lord is the Father, God. The servant is the Son, Christ Jesus. The Holy Spirit is equal love who is in them both. When Adam fell, God's Son fell; because of the faithful oneing which was made in heaven, God's Son might not part from Adam – and in Adam is understood all humankind. Adam fell from life into death into the vale of this wretched world and after that into hell. God's Son fell with Adam into the valley of the Maiden's womb, she who was the fairest daughter of Adam, in order to excuse Adam from all his blame in heaven and in earth; and then mightily he fetched him out of hell.[70] By the wisdom and goodness of the servant is to be understood God's Son. By the poor labourer's clothing and his standing near the left side is understood (Christ's) manhood and Adam, with all the mischief and feebleness that resulted; for in all this, our good Lord showed his own Son and Adam as but one man. The virtue and

---

[70] The 'harrowing of hell' – cf. ch. 13 – whereby immediately after his death on the cross Christ descends into hell to harvest the just souls from Adam through Abraham to all the saved who had waited in faith for his great deed.

the goodness that we have is of Jesus Christ, the feebleness and blindness is of Adam; both of which were shown in the servant. And so has our good Lord Jesus taken upon himself all our blame; and therefore our Father may assign, neither will he, no more blame to us, than to his own Son, dearworthy Christ. And so it was that he was the servant even before his coming into[71] the earth, who stood ready before the Father prepared against the time when he would send him to do that worshipful deed by which mankind would be brought once more into heaven; that is to say, notwithstanding that he is God, equal with the Father as regards the Godhead, he already foresaw his purpose to become man so as to save mankind in fulfilment of his Father's will, so that he stood before his Father as a servant, willingly taking upon himself all our debts.

And then he set off promptly in answer to his Father's will, and at once he fell down low into the Maiden's womb, regardless of himself or his hard pains. The white smock is his flesh; its plainness, that there is nothing between the Godhead and the manhood; its straitness, his poverty; its age comes from Adam's wearing; the staining with sweat from Adam's labours; while its shortness shows how the servant must labour.

And so I saw the Son standing, and he spoke his purpose thus: 'Lo, my dear Father, I stand before you in Adam's smock all ready to start and run my course. I wish to be in the earth to do your service whenever it is your will to send me. How long must I wait?' Full well the Son knew when it was the Father's will and how long he would wait; that is to say with respect to the Godhead, for he is the Wisdom of the Father. So that this meaning was shown of the manhood of Christ; for all those that shall be saved by the sweet Incarnation and blissful passion of Christ, they are all of the manhood of Christ: for he is the head and we are his members. Now to those members

---

[71] 'into' rather than 'onto': Julian has her example vividly before her eyes — the servant falling into the earthly vale, the Son falling into the Maiden's womb.

the day and the time is not known when every passing woe and sorrow shall come to an end and their everlasting joy and bliss shall be fulfilled; yet all the company of heaven long to see that day and its time. And for all those still under heaven who are yet to come thither, their way also is by longing and desire; this is the same longing that was shown in the servant standing before his lord; and again in the Son standing before the Father in Adam's smock; for the languor and desire of all mankind that shall be saved appeared in Jesus; for Jesus is all that shall be saved and all that shall be saved is Jesus. And all is of the charity of God, with obedience, meekness and patience and the virtues that belong to us.

Also in this marvellous parable, I have teaching set before me, just like the beginning of an ABC, whereby I may have some understanding of our Lord's meaning. For all that is hidden about this revelation is contained therein, notwithstanding all the revelation is full of secrets.

Having understood this much, Julian seems content to admit that she will never understand the showings in their fullest meaning. She now sums up what she has understood.

The sitting of the Father is token of his Godhead, that is to say, it shows rest and peace; for in the Godhead there may be no labour. And he showed himself as lord in token of our manhood. The standing of the servant betokens travail; being to one side and on the left is token of his unworthiness to stand an equal before his lord. His starting was the Godhead and his running was the manhood; for the Godhead starts from the Father into the Maiden's womb, falling into the taking of our kind; and in this falling he took great hurt; the hurt he took was the flesh in which he also had such feeling of deadly pains. In that he stood in dread before the lord, not straight in front of him, is token that his clothing was not honest to standing straight in front of the lord. Nor could that, nor should that be his place while he was still a servant; neither might he sit at rest and peace with the lord until he had won his peace by right with his hard travail. And by the left-hand side is meant that the Father allowed his Son, willingly, to suffer in his manhood many pains without sparing him. And by his smock being almost in rags and tatters is understood the rods and scourges, the thorns and nails, the drawing and the dragging, that rent his tender flesh. As I saw to some degree, his flesh was rent from the top of his head, falling in pieces until the time the bleeding ceased; and then it began to dry again, clinging to the bone. And by the wallowing and writhing, groaning and moaning, it is understood that he might never rise almightily from the time he had fallen into the Maiden's womb till his body was slain and dead; when he yielded his soul into the Father's hands with all humankind for whom he had been sent.

And at this point, he first began to show his might. For he went into hell, and when he was there he raised the great root out of the deep, depths which rightfully were knit to him in high heaven. His body was in the grave until the Easter morrow, and from that time he never lay no more; for then truly was an end to the wallowing and writhing, the groaning and moaning; and our foul mortal flesh that God's Son took upon himself, which was Adam's old smock, strait, threadbare and short, then by our Saviour was made fair: now white, bright and of endless cleanness, wide and full, more fair, more rich than the clothing which I saw on the Father. For that clothing was blue and Christ's clothing is now fine and dazzling, a many-colour mix so marvellous it may not be described, it is so worshipful.

Now the Lord no longer sits upon the earth in a wilderness, but he sits in his most noble throne which he made in heaven most to his liking. Now the Son no longer stands before the Father in awe like a servant, poorly clothed, part naked; but he stands before the Father an equal, richly clad in generous bliss, and with a crown upon his head of precious richness; for it was shown that we are his crown, which is the Father's joy, the

Son's glory, and a liking to the Holy Spirit, and an endless marvellous bliss to all who are in heaven.

Now the Son stands no more before the Father to his left side like a labourer, but he is seated on his Father's right hand in endless rest and peace. But this is not to mean that the Son sits on the right hand, side by side, as a man may sit beside his wife in this life: for there is no such sitting, as I see it, in the Trinity; but he sits on the Father's right hand, that is to say, in the highest nobility of the Father's joys. Now is the spouse, God's Son, in peace with his beloved wife who is the fair Maiden of endless joy. And now the Son sits, true God and man, in his city of rest and peace, which his Father has prepared for him in his endless purpose: and the Father in the Son, and the Holy Spirit in the Father and the Son.

52

As if liberated by the successful outcome of this lengthy parable,
Julian is now free to talk about the inner workings of mercy and grace
that come about as a result of Adam's — and our own — falling.

AND thus it was I saw that God rejoices that he is our Father, God rejoices that he is our Mother, and God rejoices that he is our true Spouse and our soul his beloved wife. And Christ rejoices that he is our brother, and Jesus rejoices that he is our Saviour.[72]

These are five high joys, as I understand, in which he wills that we rejoice, him praising, him thanking, him loving, him

---

[72] Julian's powerful summary of her insights into the economy of the Trinity in God's dealings with the human soul sings out with a simple authority that far outstrips mere theological statements. Compare her simple paean of Father, Mother and Spouse to *The Catechism of the Catholic Church* (Geoffrey Chapman), pp. 257–260: 'The Trinity'.

endlessly blessing. All that shall be saved have during their time of life a strange medley of both weal and woe. We have in us our Lord Jesus risen: we have in us the wretchedness and mischief of Adam's falling. In this dying we are steadfastly kept by Christ, by his grace that continually touches us, and so are we raised into the sure hope of our salvation.[73] And by our falling in Adam, we are so broken in our feelings, in different ways, by sins and sundry pains, in which we are made dark and blind so that we may scarcely find any comfort. But in our intention, we await God, faithfully trusting him to have mercy and give us his grace; for this is his own working within us. And of his goodness, he opens the eye of our understanding so that we may see, sometimes more, sometimes less, according as God gives us ability to receive it. And now we are raised into weal, now we are allowed to fall into woe. And so strange is the mingling of the two within us that we scarce know for ourselves or for our fellow Christians how it stands with us, because of this strange mixture of feelings.[74] But each holy assent that we offer God when we feel him truly, willing to be with him with all our heart, with all our soul and with all our might, enables us to hate and despise those evil stirrings as well as all occasion of sin both in spirit and body. Nevertheless, once this sweetness is hidden, we fall again into blindness, so that woe and tribulation follow in various ways. But then we must take this comfort, for we know in faith that by the power of Christ, who is our keeper, we never assent thereto. Rather we complain against them and bear the pain and woe, praying for the time when he will show himself to us again. And so it is we stand in the midst of this mingling all the days of our life. But he wants us to trust that he is with us all the while. For so he is in three ways: he is with us in heaven, true man drawing

---

[73] We already possess our salvation in this mortal life in sure hope by the power of the Holy Spirit (Romans 15.13).

[74] Discernment of spirits, the art of interpreting these fluctuations, has been a constant source of debate among spiritual directors both before Julian's day and ever since.

us up into his own person (and this was shown by his spiritual thirst); and he is with us too on earth leading us on (and this
was shown in the third revelation where I saw God in a point);
and he is with us within our soul endlessly dwelling, ruling and
caring for us (and this was shown in the sixteenth revelation,
as I shall say).

And so in the servant was shown the mischief and blindness
caused by Adam's falling; and in the servant was also shown the
wisdom and goodness of God's Son. And in the lord was shown
the compassion and pity of Adam's woe; and in the lord was
shown the high nobility and endless honour that humankind is
come to by the power of the passion and death of God's most
dear Son. On account of which he greatly rejoices in his
falling75 because of the great raising and fullness of bliss that
mankind is come to, far surpassing what would have been ours
had we never fallen. It was to see this surpassing nobility that
my understanding was led by God in the time I saw the servant
fall. And now because of this, we have ground for mourning,
for our sin is the cause of Christ's pains; and we also have lasting reason for joy, for his everlasting love made him suffer. And
there the creature that sees and feels the working of his love by
grace hates nothing but sin alone. For of all things, by my reckoning, love and hate are the hardest and most irreconcilable
opposites. And notwithstanding all this, I saw and understood
in our Lord's meaning that in this life we may not keep ourselves from sin as holy and fully clean as we will in heaven. But
we may still keep ourself, by grace, from sins that would lead
us to endless pains, as holy Church teaches us, and leave aside
venial sins, minding them with all our might. And if by our
blindness and wretchedness we have fallen, then we readily rise
up, knowing the sweet touch of grace and with good will
repent us according to the teaching of holy Church, according

---

75 I.e. into the Maiden's womb (ch. 51); and also Adam's falling without
which we would not be lifted up even higher – O felix culpa, the 'fortunate sin'
sung out in the Easter Night vigil.

as the sin is grievous, and go forward again to God in love. And neither on the one hand falling over low and inclining to despair, nor on the other hand being over reckless and as if we gave no thought; but openly recognizing our feebleness, knowing that we may not stand for a twinkling of an eye without being kept in grace, and reverently clinging to God, trusting only in him. For God beholds things this wise; humans see things otherwise. For it belongs to us meekly to accuse ourselves; and it belongs to the property of the goodness of our Lord God courteously to excuse us.

And these were the two parts that were shown in the twofold gaze with which the lord beheld the fall of his beloved servant. One was shown outwardly, most meekly and mildly with the great compassion and pity that comes of his endless love. And our Lord wills that we accuse ourselves in this very way, knowingly and truthfully, recognizing and knowing our falling and all the harm that comes thereof, seeing and knowing that we may never restore it; and withal willing and truly seeing and knowing the everlasting love he has for us, that all is of his plentiful mercy. And to see and know both parts together, by his grace, is the meek accusing that our Lord asks of us, and he himself works it where it is; that is to say, in the lower part of our life, as was shown in his outer regard. And in this showing, I saw two parts: one is mankind's pitiful falling; the other is the glorious satisfaction he has made for us. The other regard was inward and that was of a much higher kind and all one; for the life and power that we have in the lower part is of the higher, and it comes down by the natural self-love we have by grace. And between these two there is no division, but all is one and the same love. And this blessed love has a twofold working; for in the lower part there are pains and passions, pity, mercies and forgiveness and other such helps; but in the higher part there are none of these, for here all is high love and marvellous joy, in which marvellous joy all pains are wholly destroyed. And in this our good Lord showed not only our excusing, but also the glorious

nobility he will bring us to, turning all our blame into endless
worship.

53

Julian's longstanding difficulty about the nature of sin is answered.
In every soul that is saved there is a godly will that never consents to sin.
For when God made our soul, it was from nothing.
So we are held in our making one with our Maker and always will be.
'By the endless assent of all the Trinity,
the Second Person would be the ground and head of this fair nature.
From him we all come, in him we are all enclosed,
into him we are all going; and in him we will find our full heaven.'

AND I saw that it is his will that we understand how he takes
it no harder when a creature that shall be saved falls than
he took it when Adam fell; whom we know was endlessly loved and surely kept in the time of all his need and now
is blissfully restored in high, surpassing joys. For our Lord God is
so good, so gentle and so courteous that he may never apportion
blame to those in whom he will ever be blessed and praised.

And in this that I have just said my desire was answered, in
part, and my great difficulty eased somewhat by the lovely and
gracious showing of our good Lord. In this showing, I saw and
understood full surely that in every soul that shall be saved is a
godly will that never assents to sin, nor ever shall. Moreover
this will is so good that it may never will evil but evermore and
continually it wills good and works only good in the sight of
God. Therefore our Lord wills us to know this in faith and
belief; and namely and truly that we have all this blessed will
whole and safe in our Lord Jesus Christ. For by God's right-
eousness, all humankind, that will one day fulfil heaven, needs
to be knit and oned to him in such a way that therein is a

substance which might never, nor should ever be parted from him; and all this is through his own good will and by his endless foreseeing purpose. And notwithstanding this rightful knitting and this endless oneing, yet the redemption and again-buying of mankind is needful and speedful*[76] in its every aspect, being done by the same intent and for the same end that holy Church teaches us in our faith.

For I saw that God never began to love humankind; for inasmuch as humankind shall be in endless bliss, bringing to fulfilment God's joy in his works, so also humankind has been, in the foresight of God, known and loved from without beginning, according to his rightful plan. And by the endless assent and full accord of all the Trinity, the Second Person would be the ground and head of this fair nature. From him we all come, in him we are all enclosed, into him we are all going; and in him we will find our full heaven in everlasting joy by the foreseeing purpose of the blessed Trinity from without beginning.

For before he made us, he loved us; and when we were made, we loved him; and this love comes of the kindly substantial goodness of the Holy Spirit, mighty by reason of the power of the Father, wise in the mind of the wisdom of the Son. And thus the human soul is made of God and in the same point is knit to God. And thus I understand that the soul is made of nothing, that is to say, it is made but not from anything that is made. It is like this: when God would make the body, he took the slime of the earth, that is material which is mixed and gathered of all material things, and in this way he made our body. But as to the making of our soul, he took nothing: he simply made it. And so is our made-nature rightfully oned with its Maker, who is substantial nature, un-made: that is, God.[77] And so it is that there can, nor shall be, nothing

---

[76] Julian is stating that it was not sufficient that Christ became man ('rightful knitting'): his passion ('again-buying') was expedient and necessary.

[77] This account of our 'making' lies at the heart of Julian's experience of God's courteous love for us: in our very making we are oned to the Trinity.

between God and our soul. And in this endless love is our soul kept whole, as the letter of the revelations and their meaning shows. And in this endless love we are led and kept by God and never shall be lost. For he wills us to know that our soul is alive and this life, of his goodness, and by his grace, shall last unto heaven without end, him loving, him thanking, him praising. And just as we are to be without end, so were we treasured in God, and hidden, known and loved without beginning.

Therefore he wants us to know that the noblest thing that ever he made is humankind; and the fullest substance and the highest power is the blessed soul of Christ. And furthermore he wills us to know that all the souls that shall be saved in heaven without end are knit in this knot and oned in this oneing, and made holy in this holiness.

54

*'We ought to take great joy that God dwells in our soul,
and even more joy that our soul dwells in God ...
our faith is a power that comes from our kind substance into our sensual
soul by the Holy Spirit, by which power he comes to us.'*

AND because of the great, endless love God has for all humankind, he makes no distinction in the love he has for the blessed soul of Christ and the least soul that shall be saved. For it is very easy to believe and trust that the dwelling of the blessed soul of Christ is full high in the glorious Godhead. Yet in truth, as I understand our Lord to mean, where the blessed soul of Christ is, there too is the substance of all souls that are to be saved by Christ.

We ought to take great joy that God dwells in our soul, and even more joy that our soul dwells in God. Our soul is made to be God's dwelling place, and the dwelling place of the soul is God, that is unmade. And here is a high understanding, inwardly to see and to know that God, who is our Maker, dwells in our soul. And a higher understanding yet is to see and know that our soul, which is made, dwells in God's substance: of which substance we are all that we are. And I saw no difference between God and our substance, but as it were all God, and yet my understanding took it that our substance is in God, that is to say, that God is God, and our substance is a creature in God.

For the almighty truth of the Trinity is our Father, for he made us and keeps us in him; and the deep wisdom of the Trinity is our Mother in whom we are all enclosed; and the high goodness of the Trinity is our Lord and in him we are enclosed and he in us. We are enclosed in the Father, and we are enclosed in the Son, and we are enclosed in the Holy Spirit. And the Father is enclosed in us, and the Son is enclosed in us, and the Holy Spirit is enclosed in us: all might, all wisdom, all goodness, one God, one Lord.

And our faith is a power that comes from our kind substance into our sensual soul by the Holy Spirit,[78] by which power he comes to us – for without that, no one receives such gifts. For it is nothing else but a right understanding, with true belief and sure trust, of our very being: that we are in God, and God in us (yet this we may not see). And this power with all else that God has ordained for us coming from it, works great things in us. For it is Christ's mercy working in us, and we are by grace brought ever closer in accord with him through the gifts and the power of the Holy Spirit; this continual working is making us into Christ's children, Christian in our living.

---

[78] Julian explains that our faith (which belongs essentially to our inner reality) is rooted in our humanity (kind); we have knowledge of our sensual soul by touchings of the Holy Spirit.

55

'So was my understanding led by God to see in him and understand,
to learn and to know of him that our soul is a made trinity,
like to the un-made blessed Trinity,
known and loved from without any beginning;
and in the making it is oned to the Maker.'

AND thus Christ is our way, leading us surely in his laws, and Christ in his body mightily bears us up into heaven. For I saw that Christ, having in himself all of us that shall be saved by him, worshipfully presents his Father in heaven with us; which present his Father receives very thankfully and courteously gives it to his Son, Jesus Christ. So that this gift and working is joy to the Father and bliss to the Son and liking to the Holy Spirit. And of all things that belong to us, it is most pleasing to our Lord that we rejoice in this joy which is in the blessed Trinity concerning our salvation.

And this was seen in the ninth showing, where it speaks more of this matter. And in spite of our feelings of weal and woe, God wants us to understand and have faith that we are more truly in heaven than on earth. For our faith comes from the kind love of our soul and from the clear light of our reason and from the steadfast mind which we have from God in our first making. And at the same time that our soul is breathed into our body, when we are made sensual, then at once mercy and grace begin their workings, caring and keeping us in pity and love. In this same working, the Holy Spirit forms, in our faith, hope that we shall come again up above to our substance, into the power of Christ, grown and fulfilled in the Holy Spirit.

Thus I understood that the sensuality is grounded in kind, in mercy and in grace; it is this ground that enables us to receive those gifts that lead us to endless life.[79] For I saw quite clearly

---

79 Julian again (see chs. 19 and 22) explores her teaching of the two wills, and on into the next chapter.

that our substance is in God; also that in our sensuality, God is: for the selfsame point that our soul is made sensual, in that point is the city of God, ordained for him from without beginning. Into which city, he comes and never shall remove from there, for God is never out of the soul in which he shall dwell blissfully without end. And this was seen in the sixteenth showing, where it says: 'Jesus takes his place in our soul and he shall never remove from there.' And all the gifts that God may give to creatures, he has given to his Son Jesus for us; and these gifts he, dwelling in us, has enclosed in him until the time we are full grown and mature, our soul with our body and body with soul, each helping the other until we have reached our full stature that our kind works. And then, in the ground of our kind, by the working of mercy, the Holy Spirit graciously inspires into us his gifts leading us to endless life.

And so was my understanding led by God to see in him and understand, to learn and to know of him that our soul is a made trinity, like to the un-made blessed Trinity, known and loved from without any beginning; and in the making it is oned to the Maker, as has already been said. This was a most sweet sight and marvellous to behold, where there was peace and rest, certainty and much delight. And because of the worshipful oneing that was thus made by God, between the soul and the body, it follows that human nature must be restored from a double death. This restoring might never take place until the time the Second Person of the Trinity had taken the lower part of our nature, to whom that higher part was oned in the first making. And both these parts were in Christ, the higher and the lower; which is but one soul. The higher part was one in peace with God in fullest joy and bliss; the lower part, which is sensuality, suffered for the salvation of mankind.

And these two parts were seen and felt in the eighth showing, in which my body was filled full of feeling and remembrance of Christ's passion and his death. And furthermore, with this came a subtle feeling and secret inner sight of the high part that I was shown at the time, where I might not, for I was offered my intermediary,[80] look up to heaven. And that was because of that mighty beholding of the inner life; this inner life is that high being, that precious soul which is endlessly in its joying in the Godhead.

56

'Our soul is kindly rooted in God in endless love.'

AND thus I saw most surely that we more readily come to the knowing of God than to that of our own soul; for our soul is so deeply grounded in God, and so endlessly treasured, that we may not come to know it until first we know God, which is the Maker to whom it is oned. But notwithstanding, I saw that, for the fulfilling and perfecting of our nature, we must desire wisely and truly to know our own soul, by which we are taught to seek it where it is, that is, in God. And so by the gracious leading of the Holy Spirit we shall know them both in one; whether we are stirred to know God or our own soul, both promptings are good and true.

God is nearer to us than our own soul; for he is the ground in whom our soul stands, and he is the mean that keeps the substance and sensuality together, so that they shall never part. For our soul sits in God in very rest and our soul stands in God for very strength and our soul is kindly rooted in God in endless love.[81] And therefore if we wish to know our soul and

---

[80] Julian refused to look up to heaven, although she felt about to die; instead, her prompting was to fasten her gaze upon her intermediary, her suffering Saviour. She offers us her mystical glimpse of the oneing of the substance and the sensual in Christ's passion that she herself suffered as she refused to look up to heaven (cf. ch.19).

[81] This single apophatic phrase might be the best sum of all that Julian has to tell.

have communing and dalliance therewith, we will need to seek into our Lord God in whom it is enclosed. And I understood more about how it is enclosed in the sixteenth showing, as I will explain.

And as regards our substance, it may rightly be called our soul; and as regards our sensuality, it may rightly be called our soul: that is because they are both made one in God. The worshipful city that our Lord Jesus sits in is our sensuality in which he is enclosed; and our kindly substance is enclosed in Jesus sitting with the blessed soul of Christ at rest within the Godhead. And I saw full surely that it is our task to live in longing and in penance until the time that we are led so deep into God that we verily and truly know our own soul.

And truly I saw that into this high depth we are led by our good Lord himself in the same love with which he made us, and in the same love with which he bought us by mercy and grace through the power of his blessed passion. And notwithstanding all this, we may never come to full knowing of God until first we know our own soul. For until the time that our soul achieves its full might, we may not become all holy. This means that our sensuality, by virtue of Christ's passion, be brought up into the substance, with all the fruits of our tribulation that our Lord will award us, by mercy and grace.

I had, in part, a touching of God, and it is grounded in nature. That is to say, our reason is grounded in God, who is substantial nature. From this substantial nature mercy and grace spring and flow into us, working all things to fulfil our joy. These are our ground from which we have our increase and fulfilment; for in kind we have our life and being, and in mercy and grace we have our increase and fulfilling; these are the three properties in one goodness, and where one works, all work towards that for which we now long.

God wishes that we understand and desire with our whole heart and all our strength more and more to grow in knowledge of them until the time they are fulfilled. For to know them in full, to see them in clarity, is none other than the endless joy and bliss that we shall know in heaven; which God wills is begun here by knowing his love. For we may make no progress by reason alone; we also need to have insight and love. Nor can we be saved merely by our nature grounded in God; but coming from the same ground we also need mercy and grace. For it is by these three working together we receive all good benefits; the first of which are goods of kind. For in our first making God gave us full goods, and then he gave greater goods still, such as may only be received in our spirit; so that in his foreseeing purpose and in his endless wisdom he willed we were doubly endowed.

57

'Our Saviour is our true mother
in whom we are endlessly born yet we will never come out of him.'
Julian sums up how our substance and our sensuality, the one full,
the other failing, are taken by Christ to be reformed and restored.

REGARDING our substance, he made us noble and so rich that we may evermore fulfil his will and do him honour. And when I say we, I mean all that shall be saved; for I saw in truth that we are those whom he loves and we do his liking lastingly without stint. And from the great riches and high nobility virtues come to our soul in some measure[82] at the time when our soul is knit to our body, that is when we are made sensual.

Thus in our substance we are full, and in our sensuality we are failing; and it is this failing which God will restore and fulfil by the working of mercy and grace which flow into us plentifully from his own eternal goodness. Thus his own eternal

---

[82] Or 'by design', i.e. God's plan for us. See p. 85, footnote 64.

goodness makes mercy and grace to do their work in us; and our own substantial goodness, that we have received from him, enables the mercy and grace to work in us. For I saw that in God our kind is whole; yet he also makes diversities flow from him which do his will; they keep our kind which grace and mercy restores and fulfils. None of these shall perish, for our substance, which is the higher part, is knit to God in our making. And God is knit to the lower part of our substance when he took our flesh: and thus in Christ our two substances are oned. For the Trinity is comprehended in Christ in whom our higher part is grounded and rooted; and it is the lower part that the Second Person has taken, which nature was first prepared for him. For I surely saw that all the works that God has done, or ever shall do, were known to him in full and foreseen by him without beginning. He made humankind for love, and in the same love he wanted to become man.

The next good we receive is our faith, the source of all our benefits. And it comes down from the high riches of our human nature into our sensual soul; for it is grounded in us and we in it through God's own substantial goodness by the workings of mercy and grace. From here too come all other benefits by which we are guided and saved. Thus the commandments of God stem from here which we ought to understand in two ways: he bids us love and keep them; equally we should know his prohibitions, to hate and refuse them. The whole of our task is summed up in this twofold manner.

From faith also come the seven sacraments, each following upon the other according to the plan God has devised for us, as well as all manner of other virtues. For the same virtues that we have received from our substance, given to us in our human nature, by the goodness of God, the same virtues, by the working of mercy, are given to us in grace to be renewed through the Holy Spirit. The very same virtues are stored up for us in Jesus Christ; for in that same time that God knitted him to our body in the Maiden's womb he took our sensual soul. In this taking, having enclosed us within himself, he oned it to our substance and in his oneing became perfect man. For Christ, having knit to himself all those men and women that shall be saved, is the perfection of humankind. So is our Lady our Mother in whom we are all enclosed and of her born in Christ; for she who is mother of the Saviour, is mother too of all who will be saved in our Saviour. And our Saviour is our true Mother in whom we are endlessly born yet we will never come out of him.

All this was shown abundantly, plainly and sweetly. And it is spoken of in the first showing where he says we are all enclosed in him and he is all enclosed in us; and that is also spoken of in the sixteenth showing where it tells of him sitting in our soul. For it is his delight to reign in our understanding blissfully, and to sit in our soul peacefully, and to dwell in our soul endlessly, working us all into him. And we are his helpers in this working, attending to him all our day, learning his lore, keeping his laws, wanting all that he desires to be achieved, truly trusting him. I saw in truth that our substance is in God.

58

'I beheld the working of all the blessed Trinity.'
Julian speaks eloquently of the working of God with us.

GOD, the blissful Trinity, is everlasting Being; as surely as he is endless and without beginning, so surely was it his endless purpose to make humankind. Yet humanity's fair nature was first prepared for his own Son, the second Person: then, when the chosen time came, by full accord of all the Trinity, he made us all at once; and in our making, he knitted us and oned us to himself. And in this bond we are kept as clean and noble as at the time of our making. And, by the power of this same precious bond, we love our Maker and like him, praise him and thank him with a joy in him that has no end. This then is the task which he works continually in every soul that shall be saved all according to this said plan of God.

And so it is that in our making God almighty is Father of our substance; and God all wisdom is Mother of our substance; with the love and the goodness of the Holy Spirit; which is all one God, one Lord. In the knitting and the oneing he is our very own spouse, as we are his beloved wife and fair maiden; with his own wife he may never be displeased. For he says as much: 'I am loving you, and you are loving me: and our loving shall never be parted in two.'

I beheld the working of all the blessed Trinity, and in this beholding I saw and understood these three properties: the property of fatherhood, the property of motherhood, and the property of the Lordship in one God. In our Father almighty we have our keeping and our bliss as regards our human substance, which is ours by our making without beginning. And in the Second Person, in wit and wisdom, we have our keeping as regards our sensuality, our restoring and our saving: for he is our Mother, Brother and Saviour. And in our good Lord the Holy Spirit we have our rewarding and our recompense for our living and our labours which will far exceed anything we can desire, owing to his marvellous courtesy and his high plenteous grace.

For our whole life is in three.[83] In the first we have our being, and in the second we have our increasing, and in the third we have our fulfilling. The first is kind, the second is mercy and the third is grace. In the first, I saw and understood that the high might of the Trinity is our Father; and the deep wisdom of the Trinity is our Mother; and the great love of the Trinity is our Lord: and all this we have and own in our natural kind and in the making of our substance.

---

[83] In one of her finest chapters, Julian is boldly wrestling with the unsayable: how the economy of the Trinity impinges upon our reality and our experience of that reality.

And more than this, I saw that the Second Person, who is Mother of our substance, the same most dear Person is become our Mother sensual. For we are doubly of God's making: that is to say, substantial and sensual. It is our substance that is the higher part, this we have in our Father, God almighty; and the Second Person of the Trinity is Mother in nature, in our substantial making, in whom we are grounded and rooted; and he is also our Mother in mercy in taking our sensuality. And so our Mother works in diverse ways for us, so that our parts are held together. For in our Mother Christ we profit and increase as in mercy he reforms and restores us, while, by the power of his passion and his death and rising, he ones us to our substance. And so our Mother works in such a merciful way with all his children, making them buxom and obedient.

And grace works alongside mercy, that is to say in two properties, as was shown; as for this working, it belongs to the Third Person, the Holy Spirit. He works by rewarding and giving: rewarding is a generous gift of truth which the Lord gives to those who have laboured; while giving is a courteous working which he freely performs by his grace, overpassing all that a creature deserves.

Thus in our Father, God almighty, we have our being; and in our Mother of mercy we have our reforming and restoring, and in him our parts are oned and we all made perfect human beings; and by the recompense and giving in grace of the Holy Spirit we are fulfilled. And our substance is our Father, God almighty, and our substance is our Mother, God of all wisdom, and our substance is in our Lord the Holy Spirit, God of all goodness; yet our substance is whole in each Person of the Trinity, which is one God. While our sensuality is only in the Second Person, Christ Jesus, yet in him is the Father and the Holy Spirit. And in him and by him we are mightily taken out of hell and out of this wretchedness on earth, and gloriously brought up into heaven and blissfully oned to our substance, with every increase in riches and nobility, all by the power of Christ and by the grace and working of the Holy Spirit.

59

*The refrain 'I it am' now repeats
to tell the working of the Trinity in mercy and grace.
Christ mothers us in kind by our first making and in grace by taking our
flesh as his own.*

AND all this bliss we have by mercy and grace. Nor might we ever have known it in such manner had not the very property of goodness which is in God been opposed; on this account alone do we have our bliss. For wickedness has been allowed to rise against goodness, and the goodness of mercy and grace prevailed against the wickedness, turning it all to goodness and glory for all them that shall be saved; for it is the property of God to do good against evil.

Since Jesus Christ does good against evil, he is our true Mother; for we have our being of him where the ground of motherhood begins, with all the sweet keeping of love that follows endlessly. Even as rightly God is our Father, so is God rightly our Mother; and this he showed in all, and especially in these sweet words where he says: 'I it am'.[84] That is to say:

I it am: the might and the goodness of the Fatherhood.
I it am: the wisdom of the Motherhood.
I it am: the light and the grace that is all blessed Love.
I it am: the Trinity.
I it am: the Unity.
I am the sovereign goodness of all manner of things.
I am that makes you to love.
I am that makes you to long.
I it am: the endless fulfilling of all true desires.

For then the soul is highest, noblest and most worthy when

---

[84] This passage is a development of what has gone before in a specifically trinitarian mode: cf. ch. 26 for the first 'I it am' showing.

it is lowest, meekest and mildest. And from this substantial ground we have all our virtues and our sensuality by the gift of nature and by the help and quickening of mercy and grace without which we can make no progress.

Our high Father, God almighty, who is Being, he knew us and loved us from before time; and from his knowing, in his marvellous deep charity by the foreseeing endless counsel of all the blessed Trinity, he willed that the Second Person should become our Mother, our Brother, our Saviour. And from this it follows that as truly as God is our Father, so truly is God our Mother. Our Father wills, our Mother works, our good Lord the Holy Spirit confirms. And therefore it is up to us to love our God in whom we have our being, reverently thanking and praising him for our making, mightily praying to our Mother of mercy and pity, and to our Lord the Holy Spirit for help and grace. For in these three is all our life – kind, mercy, grace. For from them will we know meekness, mildness, patience and pity; then we will hate sin and wickedness.

And thus Jesus is our true Mother in kind, by our first making; and he is our true Mother in grace by his taking our kind that is made. All the fair working and all the sweet kindly office of dearworthy motherhood are appropriated to the Second Person. For in him we have this godly will whole and safe without end, both in kind and in grace, all of his own goodness that is his alone.

I understand three ways of beholding the motherhood of God: the first is grounded in the making of our kind; the second is his taking our kind, and then begins the motherhood of grace; the third is the motherhood of working, and there begins his going forth, by the same grace, all the length and breadth, to every height and in all depths without end. And it is all of his own love.

60

Julian develops the theme of Christ's Motherhood:
not only does he mother us as our 'again-buyer' and Saviour,
but his working is also seen in our human experience of parenting.
This was shown in those mysterious, rich words :
'I it am that you love.'

BUT now it is necessary to say a little more about this 'forth-spreading':[85] as I understand it in our Lord, it means how we are brought again by the motherhood of mercy and grace into our natural home where first we were made by the motherhood of kind love, and this kind love, it will never leave us.

Our kind Mother, our gracious[86] Mother, for he would be wholly our mother in every way, he took up the ground of his work at its lowest point, in the Maiden's womb, with utter meekness. And this he showed in the first revelation, where he brought my understanding to see her in simple guise, a modest maid, just as she was when she conceived. This is to say that our high God who is sovereign wisdom of all, arrayed himself in this low place, clothing himself in our poor flesh, so that he might himself perform the service and office of motherhood in all things.

The mother's task is nearest, readiest and most sure, for it is the most real truth. This task might never, nor could it, be done

---

[85] Here speaks Julian the theologian. Contemporary experts (among whom she would not number herself) would speak of *circuminsessio* (lit. the sitting around, perhaps the seating arrangements), our clumsy essay at describing how the three distinct Persons relate internally, within themselves, and externally, with humankind. Julian uses the image of motherhood to explore the way the Second Person's intervention into the human sphere is 'spread-forth'. As always, her language is homely, direct and meaningful.

[86] 'kind' and 'gracious': natural and built-upon-nature. Julian chooses her words: Christ's motherhood begins in our nature and it continues in the workings of grace to refashion – a theme she began to develop at the end of the last chapter.

by anyone other than himself. We well know that all our
mothers bear us to pain and to dying. Yet what does he do ?
Our own true Mother Jesus, he who is all love, bears us to joy
and endless living – blessed may he be! Thus he sustains us
within himself in love and labour until the full time when he
gladly suffered the sharpest throes and most grievous pains that
ever were or ever shall be, and died at last.

And when he had done, and so borne us to bliss, yet all this
still could not satisfy his marvellous love. This he showed in
these high words of overriding love: 'If I might suffer more, I
would suffer more.' he might not die again, yet he would never
cease his working. And therefore he is compelled to feed us, for
the precious love of his motherhood makes him a debtor to us.
The mother may suckle her children with her own milk, but our
precious Mother Jesus, he may feed us with himself. And he does
this most courteously, with much tenderness, with the Blessed
Sacrament that is our precious food of true life. And with all
the sweet sacraments he sustains us with every mercy and grace.

He meant as much when he spoke these blessed words: 'I it
am that holy Church teaches you and speaks of'; that is to say:
'All the health and life of the sacraments, all the power and grace
of my word, all the good that is ordained in the Church for you,
I it am.'

The mother may lay the child tenderly to her breast, but our
tender Mother Jesus, he may lead us homely into his blessed
breast by his sweet open side and show there in part the
Godhead and the joys of heaven, with spiritual certainty of endless bliss. This was shown in the tenth revelation, giving the
same understanding by these sweet words that were said: 'Lo,
how I love you', as he gazed down into his side, with utmost joy.

This fair word full of love, mother, it is so sweet and so kind[87]

---

[87] 'sweet' and 'kind': in retaining Julian's words we need care in safeguard-
ing their meaning: 'sweet' she reserves especially to Christ, describing his loving actions; 'kind', we well know, is 'belonging to our nature'. Thus, 'sweet'
and 'kind' is Christ's all embracing love-mothering that belongs to him alone
– to his self.

and comes from the self so that it may not in truth be said but only of him, and of her who is true mother of him and of all.

The property of true motherhood is kind love, wisdom and knowing, and it is good.[88] Albeit our bodily birth is but little, low and simple when compared to our spiritual birth, yet it is he that does it in the creatures by whom it is done. The earthly mother lovingly understands her child and sees its every need; she keeps it most tenderly, for such is the true nature and condition of motherhood. Then as it grows older, her working changes, but never her love. For when it is older still, she allows it to be chastised so as to break down its vices and so help the child receive virtues and graces.

This same work, with all that may be fair and good, our Lord himself does through those by whom it is done. So he is our true Mother in kind by the working of grace in the lower part, by love in the higher part. And he wants us to know this; for he will have all our love fastened to him. And in this I saw that all our debt that we owe, at God's bidding,[89] to fatherhood and motherhood, and for God's own Fatherhood and Motherhood, are fulfilled by our true loving of God. And this blessed love Christ works in us.

And this was shown in all the revelations and especially in those mysterious, rich words when he says: 'I it am that you love.'

---

[88] 'good', i.e. Godly: motherhood in all its aspects signals God's working. Julian lists the appropriate attributes of the Trinity in motherhood – kind love, wisdom and knowing: yet it is Christ who is properly our Mother.

[89] The commandment 'honour thy father' etc. is doubly bound upon us: we owe honour to earthly and heavenly fathers. Yet Julian not only broadens the command to 'include' motherhood, she sees Christ's working immanent to the entire business of mother and father as we experience it – which leads us to appreciate his 'love in the higher part'.

61

Christ's spiritual motherhood is the more tender:
so he makes us love all that he loves for his love's sake,
lovingly calling our name and touching us by grace.

IN our spiritual birth, he uses more tenderness of keeping, without likeness, for our soul is more precious in his sight. He kindles our understanding, he directs our ways, he eases our conscience, he comforts our soul, he lightens our heart; all this that he may give us our knowing and loving, in part, of his blissful Godhead, by gracious coming to mind of his sweet manhood and his blessed passion, with a courteous marvelling in his high, overwhelming goodness. And so he makes us love all that he loves for his love's sake; he sees that we are well paid by him and all his works. As soon as we fall, he promptly raises us, lovingly calling our name and touching us by grace. And when we have been strengthened thus by his sweet working, then we gladly choose him, by his sweet grace, to be his servants and his lovers lastingly without end. And after this he suffers some of us to fall more hard and grievously than ever before, or so it seems to us. And then in our ignorance we think that all we had begun is undone. But it is not so; for it is necessary that we fall and this we need to see. For if we did not fall, we would never know how feeble and how wretched we are by ourselves. Nor would we know in such great measure the marvellous love of our Maker. For we will see truly in heaven without end that we have sinned grievously in this life; and notwithstanding this, we will also see that we were never hurt in his love, nor were we ever less prized in his sight. But by the test of this failing, we shall have a high and marvellous knowing of love in God without end. For rocklike and marvellous is that love which may not, nor will not, be broken in transgression.

And this is one meaning of our advantage. Another is the

humility and meekness we will get by the recognition of our falling; we will be raised to heaven by it, which would never be possible without that meekness. And therefore we must recognize this, for if we fail to see it, though we fall, it will profit us not.

Usually it happens that first we fall and then we see it, both by the mercy of God. Just as a mother may allow her child to fall sometimes and be distressed in various ways for its own benefit, yet she would never let any kind of harm come to the child for the love she bears it. And even though some earthly mother might allow a child of hers to perish, our heavenly Mother, Jesus, may never suffer us to be lost, for we are his children. And he is all mighty, all wisdom and all love; and there is none but he. Blessed may he be!

But often when our falling and our wretchedness are shown to us, we are so sorely pained, so full of shame, that we scarcely know where to put ourselves. But then our courteous Mother wills us not to flee away, for nothing were further from his thoughts. For now he wants us to behave just like a child; for when a child is upset or afraid, it runs straight to its mother with all its might, crying out: 'My kind mother, my gracious mother, my dearest mother, have mercy on me. I have made myself foul[90] and unlike you; and I can never put it right without your special help and grace.' And if we do not feel ourselves at ease right away, we can be sure that he uses the skills of a wise mother. For if he sees that it will profit us more to mourn and weep awhile, this he allows with compassion and pity until the best time, all out of love. And he wants us to use the ways of a child who finds it natural to trust the love of their mother in weal and woe.

And he wishes that we hold firmly to the faith of holy Church, finding there our dearest mother in comfort of true understanding, with all the blessed community of saints. For a

---

[90] Literally, 'soiled myself': Julian is putting the words of a baby into our mouths.

person all alone may frequently be broken, or so it may seem to them, but the whole body of the Church was never broken, nor never shall be, without end. And therefore it is a sure thing, good and grace-giving, to will, meekly and mightily, to be sustained and oned to our mother, holy Church, that is Christ Jesus; for the food of mercy that is his own dearest blood and precious water is plentiful enough to make us fair and clean. The blessed wound of our Saviour is open and rejoices to heal us; the sweet, gracious hands of our Mother reach out ready and diligent about us. For in all this working he uses the skills of a kind nurse who cares for nothing but the salvation of her child. His task is to save us, a duty he delights to fulfil. And he would have us know it; for he wants us to love him sweetly and trust in him meekly and mightily.

And this he showed in his gracious words: 'I keep you full surely.'

62

God is kind in his being: he is goodness at source.
This kind he sets forth in many diverse ways, most perfectly in humankind.

AT that time, he showed our frailty and our falling, our breakings and our nothingness, our despisings and our outcastness: all possible woe, as it seemed to me, that might ever befall us in this life. Yet withal he showed his blessed might, his blessed wisdom, his blessed love, that keeps us through all this time as tenderly and as sweetly in his honour and as surely in our salvation as he does when we are most at rest and comforted. For this end, he raises us spiritually and highly in heaven, turning it all to his honour and to our joy without end. For his love never permits that we lose any time.[91] And all this stems from the innate[92] goodness of God by the working of grace.

God is kind in his being, that is to say, that goodness that is kind, it is God. He is the ground, he is the substance, he is the same thing as kindness and he is the true Father and very Mother of Kind. And all kinds he has made to flow out from him to work his will shall be restored and brought again into him by the salvation of humanity through the working of grace. For of all the kinds he has set partially in the great variety of creatures, only in humankind is it set whole and in its fullness, by virtue, beauty, goodness, in royalty and nobility and in all manner of celebration of refinement and honour. So that here we see that we are all bound to God for our kind, so too we are bound to God by grace. Here we can see that we need not seek far and wide, curious about all those other lower natures, but look to holy Church, our mother's breast; that is to say into our own soul where our Lord dwells at home. And there we shall find all, here and now in faith and in understanding, and afterwards, truly in himself, clearly and in bliss. But let no man nor woman take this individually to themselves; for it is not so: only in general is this true. For it is our precious Christ and for him alone that this fair nature was prepared, by the honour and nobility of humanity's making and for the joys and bliss of our salvation: all just as he saw, understood and knew from without beginning.

---

[91] One of the numerous special insights of Julian: all our moments, however they seem to us, are 'speeding' us forward.

[92] kind: from his substance and nature.

63

AND here we can see how it is in our true nature and kind
that we hate sin, and grace too convinces us to hate sin;
for kind is all good and fair in the self, and grace was
sent out to save kind by destroying sin and so bring again fair
kind to the blessed point from whence it came, that is God,
with more nobility and worship brought by the virtuous*
working of grace. For it shall be seen before God and all his
holy ones rejoicing without end that when our nature was tested in the fire of tribulation it was found to be without lack or
fault. Thus kind and grace are of one accord; for grace is God,
as kind is God.

He works in two different ways with single loving purpose,
neither of which operates without the other, they being insep-
arable. And when by the mercy of God and by his help we fall
into accord with kind and grace, we shall truly see that sin is
more vile and more full of pain than hell itself – without comparison. For sin is contrary to our fair kind: in so far as sin is
unclean, so is it unnatural.[93] For this is a horrible thing for the
loving soul to see that wants only to be all fair and shining in
the sight of God just as kind and grace teach.

And while we should not dwell in fear of this, yet, inasmuch
as fear may be a help, we should quietly plead our cause[94] to
our most dear Mother, and he will wash us all over with his
precious blood and make our soul full soft and mild, healing
us fully fair in the process of time, which is to his worship and
our endless joy. And he shall never cease nor stint from this sweet
fair task till all his dear children be born and brought forth. And
that he showed when his spiritual thirst was made known, his
love and his longing that shall last until the day of doom.

---

93 unkinde (unkind): ME usage of this word could be revived: to be unkind
is to act against our loving nature.

94 mekely make we our mone: is Julian's wonderful phrase.

Thus our life is grounded in our true Mother Jesus in the foreseeing wisdom that he has from without beginning, with the might of the Father and the high sovereign goodness of the Holy Spirit. For in taking our humankind he brings us life, in his blessed[95] dying upon the cross he bore us to endless life. And from that time until now, and even until Doomsday, he feeds us and helps us, according to the high sovereign kindness of his Motherhood that answers our kindly needs of childhood. Fair and sweet is our heavenly Mother in our soul's sight; precious and lovely are his gracious children in the sight of our heavenly Mother, with mildness, meekness and all the fair virtues that belong to children in kind: for a child will never despair of a mother's love; it never presumes to rely upon itself; of its nature a child will love its mother; indeed, it is natural for each to love the other. These are the fair virtues, together with many other similar, by which we serve and please our heavenly Mother.

And I took it that in this life there is no higher state than childhood, that feebleness and failing both in capacity and understanding that shall last until such time as our gracious Mother has brought us to our Father's bliss.

And then the meaning of these sweet words shall truly be made known to us: 'All shall be well, and you shall see for yourself that all manner of thing shall be well.'

And then the bliss of our Mother in Christ shall begin anew in the joys of our God: a new beginning to last without end, newly begun. Thus I understood that all his blessed children which were born out of him by kind shall be brought into him again by grace.

---

95 'blessed': originally 'sprinkled with blood' so as to save: cf. Exodus 12.13; Hebrews 13.12.

64

'And you shall come up above;
and you shall have me as your reward;
and you will be filled full of joy and bliss.'
Julian understands the nature of our death.

BEFORE this time, I had a great longing and desire, by God's
gift, to be delivered from this world and from this life.
Frequently I witnessed the woe that is here and knew the
well-being and bliss that is there. And even if there were no
other pain in this life apart from the absence of our Lord, sometimes this alone seemed to me more than I could bear. And this
made me mourn and long more eagerly, and also my own
wretchedness, sloth and very weakness made me reluctant to
live and to labour on as I knew I should.

And to all this our courteous Lord answered by way of comfort and patience: 'Suddenly you will be taken from your pain,
from all your sickness, from all this disease and from all this
woe. And you shall come up above, and you shall have me as
your reward, and you will be filled full of love and bliss. And
you shall have no more pain of any sort, no more discomfort,
nothing will you want, but all shall be joy and bliss without
end. Why should it seem hard for you to suffer a while, since
that is my will and to my honour?'

And with the words, 'suddenly you will be taken', I saw that
God rewards us for patiently waiting upon his will until the
time he has chosen, persevering in patience all through this life.
Indeed, not to know the time of our passing is a great advantage; for if someone knew when they were to die, they would
scarcely be patient until it happened. It is God's will that as long
as the soul is in the body, it should seem to us that it is always
on the point of being taken. And all our living, our languor that

we experience here, it is but a moment, so that when we are suddenly taken out of our pain and into bliss, then pain shall be no more.

At this time, I saw a body lying on the earth, a body that was heavy and ugly; without shape or form, it was like a swollen lump of stinking mire. Then suddenly, out of this body sprang a fine, fair creature, a little child fully shaped and formed, nimble and full of life, whiter than a lily; and quickly it glided up into heaven.

The swollen state of the body stands for the wretchedness of our mortal flesh, and the little tiny child stands for the cleanliness and purity of the soul. And I thought to myself: 'Within this body this fair child cannot abide; nor has any foulness from this body tainted this child.' It is far happier that we are taken from pain, rather than pain be taken from us; for if pain were taken from us, then it might come again. Therefore it is a sovereign comfort and joyous beholding for any loving soul to know that we are to be taken from pain. For in this promise I saw the marvellous compassion that our Lord has for us in our woe, and a courteous pledge of our complete deliverance, for he wants us to find comfort in our death and passing,[96] as he showed in these words: 'And you shall come up above; and you shall have me as your reward; and you will be filled full of joy and bliss.'

It is God's will that we set the point of our thought[97] on this marvellous notion as often as we may, and for as long a time as we can stay there with his grace. For it is a blessed contemplation for a soul led by God and very greatly to his honour for as long as it lasts. And when we fall once more into our heaviness and spiritual blindness, with painful feelings of inner and bodily frailties, it is God's will that we know that he has not

---

[96] *overpassing*: the word 'joy' has been added in the Paris MS which leads all translators to interpret this passage as treating of contemplative prayer. This hardly reads smoothly since Julian is treating of death and our passing on to joy and bliss.

[97] *that we setten the poynte of our thowte*: i.e. concentrate our minds.

forgotten us. This is the meaning of these words he says for our comfort: 'And you will have no more pain of any sort, no more discomfort, nothing will you want, but all shall be joy and bliss without end. Why should it seem hard for you to suffer a while, since that is my will and does me honour?'

It is God's will that we take his promises and his comforts as generally and as powerfully as we may. And he also wants us to take the discomforts of this life as lightly as we can by counting them as nothing; for the lighter we take them and the less account we shall set upon them for love of him, the less painful they will feel, and the more thanks and reward we will have because of them.

65

AND thus I understood that whatever man or woman deliberately chooses God for love in this life, they may be sure that they are loved without end; it is this endless love that works that grace within them; for God wills that we hold firm our trust that we may be sure in hope of the bliss of heaven while we are here, with just as much certainty as when we are there. And the more anticipation and joy we take in this belief, with humble reverence, the more he is pleased, as it was shown. This reverence I refer to is a holy, courteous fear of our Lord, combined with humility, so that we see God as wonderfully great and ourself as wonderfully small.

These virtues are to be had endlessly by those that love God; and they may even now be seen and felt in some degree when we feel here the gracious presence of our Lord. His presence in all things is something most to be desired, for it works a marvellous certainty when there is true faith, sure hope and great love, accompanied by a fear that is sweet and delightful.

It is God's will that I see myself as much bound to him by

love as if he had done all his deeds just for me. And every soul should think inwardly in this way about their lover: that is to say, the love of God makes such a unity among us that, when it is truly seen, no one can part themselves from another. And so our soul should come to think that God has done for it all that he has done; this was shown to make us love him and fear no one except him. For it is his will that we learn that the might of our enemy is taken into our Friend's hand; and therefore the soul that surely knows this will fear none save the one they love. Any other fear it places in the emotions or bodily sickness or else in the imagination; and therefore although we may be in so much pain, woe and discomfort that we seem able to think of nothing save our present misery, we should, as soon as we may, pass lightly over it, leaving it to one side. And why is this? Because God wants us to know that if we know him and love him and fear him reverently, we shall have peace and find great rest; and all that he does will give us great pleasure.

And our Lord showed this with the words: 'Why should it seem hard for you to suffer a while, since that is my will and does me honour?'

And now I have told you of the fifteen revelations such as God granted to give them to my mind, renewed by illuminations and touchings, I hope, of the same Spirit that showed them all. And the first of these fifteen showings began early in the morning, about the hour of four, and they lasted each following the other in proper order, showing in fair order and clearly until it was after None[98] the same day.

---

[98] Three in the afternoon.

66

AND after this the good Lord showed the sixteenth on the night following, as I shall presently tell; and this sixteenth was in conclusion and a confirmation of all fifteen. But first I must tell you about my wretchedness and blindness.

I have said at the very beginning, 'And all my pain was suddenly taken from me.' I did not have this pain, nor any grief or discomfort as long as the fifteen showings continued to last; and at the end of them, all was closed down and I saw nothing more. Soon after, I felt that I was going to live and suffer longer. And at once my sickness came on again. First, it was in my head, with a sound and a din; then suddenly my whole body was full of sickness just as it had been before. And I was barren and dry as if I had never had any comfort. And like a wretch I moaned and grieved as I felt the pains in my body and the failing of all comfort, in soul and body.

Then a religious person[100] came to me and asked me how I fared. And I said I had raved today, and he laughed aloud and heartily. And I said: 'The cross that stood before my face, I thought it bled freely.' And at these words, the person I spoke to became very serious and began to marvel. And at once I was very ashamed and astonished at my recklessness. And I thought: 'This man, who saw nothing at all, takes seriously the least word I may say.' And when I saw that he took it sadly and with such great reverence, I wept, for I was greatly ashamed and wanted to confess; but at the time I could not tell it to a priest,

---

99 Julian has some preliminaries before telling us her final revelation which follows in ch. 67.

100 'a religious person', a priest, possibly an Augustinian from the neighbouring Austin Friary just across King Street.

for I thought: 'How would a priest believe me? For I did not believe our Lord.' Yet I had believed him truly all the while I saw him and it was my will and intention to continue to do so without end, but like a fool, I let it slip from my mind.

Ah! look at what a wretch I am! This was a grave sin, a great unkindness, that in my folly, just through feeling a little bodily pain, for a while I so unwisely lost the comfort of all these blessed showings of our Lord God. So here you can see what I am in myself; yet for all this our courteous Lord did not leave me. And I lay still until night trusting in his mercy, and then I began to sleep.

And in my sleep, at the beginning, I thought the fiend had me by my throat; and he put his face very close to mine. It was like that of a young man, yet long and wondrous lean; I had never seen anything like it. Its colour was red like tiles newly fired, with black spots pitted like stains, more foul than any tile-stone. His hair was red as rust, clipped in front, the side locks hanging from his temples. He grinned at me a knowing leer, showing white teeth; so much that I thought it made him all the more ugly. There was no proper shape to his body or hands; but he held me in his paws by the throat and would have strangled me, but he could not.

This ugly showing happened as I slept, unlike any of the others. And during all this time, I trusted that I would be saved and kept by the mercy of God. And as our courteous Lord gave me grace to waken, I scarcely had any life left in me. Those who were with me saw what was happening and wet my temples, and my heart began to take comfort.

And at once a little smoke came in through the door with a great heat and a foul stink. I said: 'Benedicite Domine! Everything is on fire here!' And I imagined it was real fire that would have burnt us all to death. I asked those around me if they smelt any of the stink. But they said, no, they smelt nothing. I said again: 'Blessed be God!', for I knew well enough it was the fiend come to tempt me. And immediately I remembered what our Lord had shown me that same day, with all the faith of holy Church, for I saw them all as one, and fled there for my comfort. And at once it all vanished away, and I was brought to great rest and peace without sickness of body or fear of conscience.

67

'In the middle of that city sits our Lord Jesus, God and man,
a fair person, large in stature, highest bishop, solemnest king,
most honourable Lord.
The place that Jesus takes in our soul,
he shall never remove from it without end;
for in us is his homeliest home and his endless dwelling.'

AND then our Lord, opening my spiritual eye, showed me my soul in the middle of my heart. I saw the soul as large as if it were an endless world and as if it were a blissful kingdom. And by the details I saw therein, I understood it to be a glorious city.

In the middle of that city sits our Lord Jesus, God and man, a fair person, large in stature, highest bishop, solemnest king, most honourable Lord. And I saw him clad solemnly, worshipfully. He sits in the soul of his own right in peace and rest. And the Godhead rules and cares over heaven and earth and all that there is: sovereign might, sovereign wisdom, sovereign goodness. The place that Jesus takes in our soul, he shall never remove from it without end — as I see it; for in us is his homeliest home and his endless dwelling.

And in this he showed the pleasure he takes in the making of our soul. For as well as the Father might make a creature, and as well as the Son could make a creature, so well did the Holy Spirit will that our soul was made; and so it was done. And therefore the blessed Trinity rejoices without end in the making of our soul; for he saw from without beginning what would please him without end.

All things he made reveals his Lordship. And to explain this an example was given me at the time of a certain creature who was given to see the great nobility and the kingdoms belonging to a lord. When he had seen all the nobility beneath, he marvelled and was stirred to seek above in the high place where the lord had his dwelling. For he reasoned rightly that his dwelling would be in the most worthy place.

And so I understood truly that our soul may never rest in things that are beneath it. And when it rises up above all creatures and comes into itself, even then it may not stay there merely to behold itself. But all its beholding is to be blissfully set in God who is its Maker dwelling therein. For in our soul is his true dwelling. And the highest light and the brightest shining of this city is the glorious love of our Lord, as I see it.

And what may make us rejoice in God more than to see in him that he rejoices in us, the highest of all his works? For I saw in the same showing that if the blissful Trinity might have made the human soul any better, any fairer, any nobler than it was made, he would not have been fully pleased with the making of the human soul.

And he wants our hearts to be raised mightily above the deepness of the earth and all vain sorrows and rejoice in him.

68

'Know well, it was no raving that you saw today.
But take it and believe it and keep yourself in it
and comfort yourself with it and trust yourself to it:
and you shall not be overcome.'
And the whole of this teaching of true comfort
is spoken in general to all my fellow Christians.

THIS was a delightful sight and a restful showing: that it is
without any end. And the beholding of this while we are
here is most pleasing to God and also speeds us upon our
way. And the soul who beholds it in such a way makes itself
like to him whom it beholds, oneing itself to him in rest and
peace by his grace.

And it was a particular joy and bliss to me that I saw him
sitting; for the certainty of sitting shows him dwelling endlessly. And he gave me sure knowing that it was he who had
shown me all that went before. And when I had beheld this
with attention, then our good Lord showed me these words,
humbly, without voice or opening of lips, saying full sweetly:
'Know well, it was no raving that you saw today. But take it
and believe it and keep yourself in it and comfort yourself with
it and trust yourself to it: and you shall not be overcome.'

These final words were to teach me that it was indeed our
Lord Jesus who had shown me everything. And just as in the
first words that our Lord showed, meaning his blissful passion:
'Herewith is the fiend overcome', so too in these last words
were said in true deliberation, meaning all of us: 'You shall not
be overcome.'

And the whole of this teaching of true comfort is spoken in
general to all my fellow Christians, as I have already said, and
this is God's will. And these words: 'You shall not be overcome', were spoken very clearly and most mightily to mean
safety and comfort against all tribulations that might come. He

did not say, 'You shall not be tempted, you shall not be in travail, you shall not be distressed,' but he said, 'You shall not be overcome.'

God wants us to take heed of these words, that we may always be firm in sure hope. And he wills that we love him and like him and trust mightily in him: and all shall be well. And soon afterwards all was closed and I saw no more.

69

AFTER this the fiend came again with his heat and his stink, and kept me full busy. The stink was so vile and so painful, frightening and hard to bear as well. Also I heard chattering, it was bodily, like two people talking; and they both talked at once as if they were holding forth in parliament doing great business. But it was all soft mutterings, so I understood nothing of what they said.

And all this was driving me to despair; it seemed to me that they were scornfully imitating telling of beads,[101] gabbling them and not attending devoutly or thinking about the meaning as we owe to God in our prayers. But our Lord God gave me grace to trust in him mightily and to comfort my soul by speaking out loud just as if I were comforting someone else who was in trouble. It seemed to me that this business was unlike any daily business I knew.

And so I set my eyes steadfastly upon the same cross which had been a comfort to me once before; I gave my tongue to speak of Christ's passion, rehearsing the faith of holy Church; as for my heart, I fastened it upon God with all my trust and strength. And I thought to myself: 'You have a great business, to keep yourself in the faith, for you must not get taken by the

---

[101] That is, saying the rosary.

enemy. If you were to busy yourself in this way from now
onwards to avoid sin, that would be a good and excellent task.'
For I really thought that if I could keep safe from sin, I would
be free from all the fiends of hell and the enemies of my soul.
And so he occupied me all that night until morning about
prime. When suddenly, they were all gone, all vanished away
leaving only their stink which lingered awhile. And I scorned
him. And so I was delivered from him by the power of Christ's
passion, for that is how the fiend is overcome, as our Lord Jesus
Christ said before.

70

AND in all this blessed showing our good Lord made me
understand that the sight (of the revelations) would
pass; but the showing itself is kept by faith, with his
own good will and grace. For he left me neither sign nor
token by which to know it, yet he left me his own
blessed word and understanding of its truth, bidding me
firmly believe it. And so I do, blessed may he be! I believe
it is he, our Saviour, who showed it, and that it is the faith
he showed. And therefore I rejoice in believing it. And I am
bound to it, to all that he meant by the following words: 'Keep
yourself in it and comfort yourself with it and trust yourself to it.'

So it is that I am bound by my faith to keep it as true. For
on the very day that it was shown, once the sight had faded,
like a wretch I forsook it when I openly said that I had raved.
But then our Lord Jesus in his mercy would not let it perish,
but showed it all again to me, in my soul, more fully, and with
the blessed light of his precious love, saying these words quite
clearly and very gently: 'Know it well now, it was no raving
that you saw today.' It was as if he had said: 'Once the sight

passed, you lost it and could not keep it; but know it now, that is to say, now that you see it once more.'

This was said not just for this time but also that I might set my faith upon this ground, for he adds at once: 'But take it and believe it and keep yourself in it and comfort yourself with it and trust yourself to it: and you shall not be overcome.'

In the six words that follow, when he says 'take it', he means to fasten it faithfully in our heart;[102] for he wills that it dwell with us in faith until our life's end, and after that in the fullness of joy, willing that we have lasting trust in his blissful promises, knowing his goodness. For our faith is opposed in various ways by our own blindness and the spiritual enemy, within and without, and therefore our precious Lover helps us with spiritual sight and true teaching on many matters, within and without, so that we may know him.[103] And therefore in whatever way he instructs us, he wants us to discern him wisely, receive him sweetly and keep ourselves in him faithfully. For above the faith there is no goodness left in this life, as I see it; and beneath the faith there is no help to the soul; but only in the faith: that is where the Lord wills us to keep ourselves. And so we must keep ourselves in the faith by his goodness and his own working and, when he permits it, our faith is tested by the spiritual conflict so that we become strong. For if our faith has no conflict it would deserve no reward, as I understand our Lord's meaning.

---

[102] Here Julian firmly offers her revelations to all her 'even Christians', it never crossing her mind they are not for all of us. Her manner, as ever, is courteous.

[103] Julian refers again to discernment of spirits, or how we can discern the true promptings of the Holy Spirit. Margery Kempe asked Julian this very question and was answered: she should do all things that were to the worship of God and the profit of her fellow Christians: 'The Holy Spirit never urges a thing against charity.'

71

Julian at her most intimate and communicating.

GLAD and merry and sweet is the blissful face of our Lord as he looks[104] upon our souls. For, as ever we we live, he holds us continually in his love-longing,[105] and he wants our soul to look for him cheerfully, to give him his reward. And so I hope by his grace that he has, and will ever more so, draw in our outward looking towards his inward looking and make us all at one with him and each of us with the other, in true lasting joy that is Jesus.[106]

I understand our Lord's regard in three ways. The first is his look of suffering, such as he showed when he was here in this life, dying. And though this beholding is mournful and sorrowful, yet it is also glad and merry, for he is God. The second is his look of pity and ruth and compassion; and this he shows with sureness of keeping to all his lovers that need his mercy. And the third is his blissful look that shall last without end; and this was the most frequent and lasted longest.

And thus in the time of our pain and our woe, he shows us the look of his passion and his cross, helping us to bear it by his own blessed virtue. And in the time of our sinning, he looks on us with tenderness and pity and keeps us mightily, defending us against all our enemies. And these two are his most common looks in this life; mingling with them the third, that is his blissful look, in part like as it will be in heaven. And this is a

---

[104] The word for our Lord's look is *cher*, whence 'cheerful'. More than a mere glance, it is that ability and desire to give one's whole self to the other.

[105] Julian's phrase has all the swing of Hopkins: *for he havith us ever lifand in lovelongeing.*

[106] The Carthusian prays: 'Increase in us your mercy, Lord, so that in silent seclusion, we may acquire that placid glance that wounds your heart, and that love which through its purity allows you to be seen.'

gracious touching and sweet enlightening of the spiritual life which confirms us in faith, hope and charity, with contrition and devotion and also contemplation and all manner of true solace and sweet comforts. The blissful look of our Lord God works all this in us by grace.

72

Although the following chapters conclude and sum up the revelations, their somewhat disjointed nature would argue that they were written piecemeal over a longer period than those directly communicating and dwelling upon her message.

B UT now I must tell how I saw mortal sin in those creatures who will not perish for sin, but will live in the joy of God without end.

I saw that two opposites could never be together in the one place. The two that are most opposite are the highest bliss and the deepest pain. The highest bliss is to have him in clarity of endless life, him truly seeing, him sweetly feeling, all perfectly having in fullness of joy. So was the blessed face of our Lord shown in pity; and I saw in this that sin is the most opposite, so that as long as we be mixed up with any part of sin, we shall never see the blessed face of our Lord clearly. And the more horrible, the more grievous be our sin, the deeper for that time are we from this blissful sight. And therefore it seems to us many times that we were at risk of death, partly already in hell, for the sorrow and pain that sin causes us. And so we are dead for a time from true sight of our blissful life.

But in spite of all this, I saw truthfully that we are not dead in the sight of God, nor does ever he pass from us. Yet he will never have his full bliss in us until we have our full bliss in him, truly seeing his fair blissful face; for we are destined to this by our nature, the getting to it by grace. Thus I saw how sin is deadly for a short time in those blessed creatures who will have endless life.

And the more clearly a soul sees this blissful face by grace of loving, the more it longs to see it in its fullness. For notwithstanding that our Lord God dwells in us and is here with us, clasps us close, encloses us for tender love so that he may never leave us, and is more near to us than tongue can tell or heart can think, yet we may never cease from mourning and weeping nor longing until the time we can see him clearly in his blissful countenance.[107] For in that precious, blissful sight no woe can last nor shall weal fail us.

And in this I saw reason for mirth and reason to mourn. Reason for mirth, in that our Lord our Maker is so near to us and in us and we in him, by the sureness of his keeping of his great goodness. Reason to mourn, in that our spiritual eye is so blind and we are so borne down by the weight of our mortal flesh and the darkness of sin that we may not see our Lord God clearly in his fair blissful face. No, and because of this murkiness scarcely may we believe and trust his great love, or our own sure keeping. And so this is why I say that we can never cease our mourning and weeping. This weeping does not mean only pouring out tears by our bodily eye, but also a more ghostly understanding. This is because our soul's kindly desire is so great, so immeasurable, that if we were given for solace and comfort all the nobility that God has made in heaven and on earth, and still we did not see his own fair, blissful face, then we should never cease our mourning and our spirit's weeping. I say our pain will last until the time we see the fair blissful face of our Maker for ourselves. And if we were in all the pain that heart can think and tongue may tell, if at that time we could see his fair blissful face, then all this pain would not grieve us.

So that blissful sight puts an end to all manner of pain for

---

[107] *chere.*

the loving soul, filling it full of every kind of joy and bliss. And that was shown by the high, marvellous words where he said: 'I it am that is highest; I it am that is lowest; I it am that is all.'[108]

Three ways of knowing belong to us: the first that we know our Lord God; the second that we know ourselves, what we are of him by nature and grace; and the third that we humbly know what we ourselves are regarding our sin and feebleness. These were the three reasons why all the showing was made, as I understand.

73

ALL the blessed teaching of our Lord God was shown in three ways: namely, by bodily sight, by words formed in my understanding and by spiritual sight. The bodily visions I have described as accurately as I can; and the words, I have told exactly as our Lord showed them to me; as for the spiritual visions, I have spoken of them somehow, but I would never be able to tell them completely. And this prompts me to say more as God's grace will permit.

God showed me two kinds of sickness we have: one is the impatience or sloth by which we bear our labour and our pains with heaviness; the other is despair or fearful doubting, as I shall say later on. He showed me sin in general, in which all sins are contained, but in detail he showed none save these two. For it is these two that trouble and tempt us the most, as our Lord showed me, and so he wants us to attend to them. I speak of such men and women who for God's love hate sin and

---

[108] Cf. ch. 26, the twelfth showing: 'I it am that is highest. I it am that you love.' Here there is a difference of reading, where Paris retains 'you love', but both English MSS. read 'lowest'. This reading seems preferable as a synthesis of the earlier and fuller showing.

are prepared in themselves to do God's will. Then, by our blindness of spirit and heaviness of flesh, we are most inclined to them. Hence God's will that they be known and we should refuse them like all other sins.

And to help us, our Lord showed very humbly the patience he himself showed in his hard passion, as well as the rejoicing and gladness he took in his passion out of love. And he showed an example as to how we should bear our pains wisely and gladly, for that is greatly pleasing to him and endless gain to us. The reason we are greatly troubled by them is our ignorance of love. Although the three Persons of the Trinity are equal to each other, my soul took most to understanding their love. Yes indeed, he wills in all things that we have our beholding and our rejoicing in love. Yet we are most of all blind to knowing this. For some of us believe that God is all-mighty and may do everything, again that he is all-wisdom and can do everything, but that he is all-love and will do everything, there we hold back. And this ignorance, that is what most hampers God's lovers, in my eyes. For when we begin to hate sin and amend ourselves by the rules of holy Church, yet a fear remains that holds us back, as we look at ourselves and all our past sins, and for some of us even those sins we commit every day. For we hold not to our promises, neither do we keep that cleanness that our Lord has set us in; instead we fall many times into so much wretchedness that it is a shame to see. And when we see this, we become sorry and so heavy that we scarcely find any comfort. And this fear we sometimes mistake for humility, yet it is a foul blindness and a weakness. And we cannot despise it as we do with any other sin, for it comes from the enemy and is against truth.

For of all the properties of the blissful Trinity, it is God's will that we be most sure of and take most delight in his love; for love makes us strong and wisdom humbles us. For just as by the courteous wisdom of God, he forgives us our sin following our repentance, so also he wants us to forgive our sin in respect of our foolish dreads and these doubts that cast us down.

74

I understand four sorts of dread. One is dread of fright that overcomes a person suddenly through frailty. This dread does good, since it helps purge us just like a bodily sickness or another such pain that is not sinful; for all these sort of pains help us when they are taken patiently. The second dread is the pain that stirs and wakes us from the sleep of sin. For a time we are unable to perceive the soft comfort of the Holy Spirit until such time as we understand what is meant by this dread of pain, fear of bodily death, of our spiritual enemies. This dread stirs us to seek comfort and mercy from God and enables us to have contrition by the blissful touching of the Holy Spirit. The third is doubtful dread. Doubtful dread, inasmuch as it draws us to despair, God will have it turned in us to love by our knowledge of love; that is say, that the bitterness of doubt be turned into the sweetness of kind[109] love by grace. For it can never please our Lord when his servants doubt his goodness. And the fourth is reverent dread, for there is no dread in us pleases God more but reverent dread; which is most gentle, since the more it is had the less is it felt for sweetness of love.[110]

Love and dread are brethren; and they are rooted in us by the goodness of our Maker and they shall never be taken from us without end. We have it from our kind to love, and we have it from grace to love. And we have from kind to dread, and we have from grace to dread. It is right that we dread him as Lord and Father, just as it is right that we love his goodness. It belongs to us his servants and children to dread him for his Lordship and Fatherhood, as it belongs to us to love him for his goodness. And though this reverent dread and love cannot

---

[109] It is our very nature that we love God: Julian expands this later.

[110] Here Julian cannot help revealing herself as God's familiar by describing what to the onlooker might appear a contradiction.

be separated, they are not the same but distinct in property and in their working, yet neither may be had without the other. So that I am sure that whoever loves also dreads, even though they may hardly feel it.

All dreads other than reverent dread that come to us, even though they come under the colour of holiness, are not in reality holy. And we can tell them apart in this way: the dread that makes us flee hastily from all that is not good and fall into our Lord's breast like a child to its mother's bosom, with all our will and mind well knowing our feebleness and our great need, knowing his everlasting goodness and his blissful love, only seeking him for salvation, clinging to him in sure trust – the dread that brings all this about is kind, gracious, good and true. And all that is contrary to this is either wrong or it is mixed with wrong. This then is the remedy, to know them one from the other and to refuse the wrong. For in this life the profit we have naturally from dread, by the gracious working of the Holy Spirit, will stand in heaven before God, gentle, courteous and wholly delightful. And in this way we shall through love be homely and near God, and we shall through dread be gentle and courteous to God; both equally alike.

Let us then desire from our Lord God that we may dread him reverently and love him meekly and trust him mightily; for when we dread him reverently and love him meekly, our trust is never in vain. And the more we trust and the more mightily we do so, the more we please and honour our Lord whom we trust. And if we fail in this reverent dread and meek love – as God forbid we should – our trust will also falter at the same time. And therefore we are in great need to beg our Lord of his grace that we might have this reverent dread and meek love, by his gift, in our heart and in our working; for without this no one may please God.

75

I saw that God can do all that is necessary to us; and these three are what I say we most need: love, longing, pity.

Pity and love keep us in time of our need, and longing for that same love draws us towards heaven. For the thirst of God is to have humankind in general unto himself; by means of this thirst he has drawn all the saints who are with him now in bliss. And in gaining more living members, he continues to draw and to drink, yet ever he thirsts and more longs.

I saw three kinds of longing in God, all for the same end; and we have the same within us which also work to that one end. The first is that he longs to teach us to know him and love him for evermore, as it is fitting and speedful. The second is he longs to have us with him in his bliss, like those souls who are taken from pain to heaven. The third is to fill us full of bliss; and this will happen on the last day down to the very least; for I saw, as it is known by our faith, that the pain and sorrow will be at an end for all that will be saved. And not only will we receive the same bliss that belonged to souls in heaven before, but we will also receive a fresh and plentiful bliss that will flow from God into us and will fulfil us; these are all those good things which he has ordained to give us from without beginning, goods that are treasured and hidden in himself, for until that time a creature is not capable nor worthy to receive them.

In this we will at last see clearly the reason for everything he has done; and evermore we will see the cause of all that he has permitted. And the bliss and the fulfilment shall be so deep and so high that all creatures, for wonder and marvel at it all, will have so great and reverent a dread for God, surpassing all that has been seen and felt before, that the pillars of heaven shall tremble and quake.

But this kind of trembling and dread will have no pain; but it belongs to the worthy might of God to be looked at by his creatures in this way, trembling with dread and quaking in meekness of joy, marvelling only at the greatness of their Maker and the littleness of all that is made. And this beholding makes a creature marvellous meek and mild. Therefore it is God's will, and also it is our duty by both nature and grace, to attend and know this, desiring this sight and this working; for it leads us the right way, keeping us in true life by oneing us to God.

And as good as God is, so he is great; and as much as it belongs to his Godhead to be loved, so does it belong to his greatness to be dreaded; and this reverent dread is the fair courtesy that is in heaven before God's face. And greatly as he shall then be known and loved beyond anything we know now, so too will he be dreaded more than ever he is now. Therefore needs must all heaven and earth tremble and quake when the pillars tremble and quake.

76

I speak but little of reverent dread, for I hope it will be seen clearly by what has already been said. But I know full well that our Lord showed me no souls save those that dread him. And I know too that the soul which takes to heart the teaching of the Holy Spirit will hate sin in all its vileness and horror more than all the pains that are in hell. Therefore the soul that beholds the kindness of our Lord Jesus hates not so much hell as sin, as I see it. And therefore it is God's will that we know sin; and so as not to fall headlong into it, we should pray busily and work diligently and humbly seek good guidance. And if we should fall, then we must rise again readily, for it is the worst pain the soul may suffer to turn away for any time from God into sin.

The soul that would keep its peace, when another's sin comes to mind, should flee from it like the pains of hell, looking to God for remedy and the help to combat it. For contemplating another's sins makes, as it were, a mist to settle before the eye of the soul, so that for a time we can no longer see God's fairness, unless we look at another's sins with contrition with the other, with compassion for the other and with a holy desire for the other towards God; without this the soul is only harmed, perturbed and hindered by the experience. This much I understood in the revelation concerning compassion.

In this blessed revelation about our Lord I understood two conflicting truths: one is the greatest wisdom a creature may have in this life; the other the greatest folly. The greatest wisdom that any creature may have is to follow the will and counsel of his highest and best Friend. Now this highest Friend is Jesus. It is his will and counsel that we should set ourselves to him, homely evermore, in whatsoever state we be. For whether or no we be foul or clean, we are all the same in his loving. For in good times or bad, we must never flee from him; because we are so changing within ourselves, that we often fall into sin. And then we are either influenced by our enemy or by our own foolish blindness. Thus they might say: 'You know well enough you are a wretch, a sinner and unfaithful; for you fail to keep the commandments; often you promise our Lord to do better, and straightaway you fall again into the same thing, namely sloth and time wasting.' And this is the beginning of sin, it seems to me, especially for those who have given themselves to serve our Lord, seeking his goodness inwardly. For it makes us frightened to appear before our courteous Lord. It is then that our enemy tries to set us back with this false fear on account of our wretchedness, by means of the pain with which he threatens us. And his plan is to make us so heavy and so weary with it all that we put out of mind the fair, blissful beholding of our everlasting Friend.

77

OUR good Lord showed me the enmity of the fiend, by which I understood all that is opposed to love and to peace is from the fiend and his party. And through our feebleness and folly we must fall, yet, through the mercy and grace of the Holy Spirit, we are able to rise up again with even more joy. And if our enemy wins anything from our falling, for such is his liking, he loses far more when we rise up again by love and meekness. And this glorious rising causes him great sorrow and pain, for the hatred he has for our soul makes him burn continually with envy. And all this sorrow that he would make us have turns back upon himself. That is why our Lord scorned him; and it made me laugh mightily.

This then is the remedy: that we be aware of our wretchedness and flee to our Lord; for the greater be our need, the more speedily must we come near him. And we could sum up our state in these words: 'I know well that I have a sharp pain, but our Lord is all-mighty and is able to punish me mightily, and he is all-wise and knows how to punish me skilfully, and he is all goodness and loves me with every tenderness.' And we need to stay awhile and behold this; for it is loving meekness in a sinful soul, brought about by mercy and grace in the Holy Spirit, when we gladly and willingly accept the scourge and chastisement that our Lord himself decides to give us. And it will be very tender and most easy, if we will only hold ourselves content with him and all that he does. For the kind of penance we take upon ourselves was not shown to me, at least it was not shown specifically. But it was shown clearly, and shown with a look of gladdest love, that we shall meekly and patiently bear and suffer the penance that God himself gives us, remembering his own blessed passion. For when we have in mind his passion, with pity and love, then we suffer with him, just as his friends did who saw it for themselves. And this was shown in the thirteenth revelation, near the beginning, where it spoke of pity; these were his words: 'Do not accuse yourself overmuch, nor imagine that all your troubles and woe are because of your trespasses; for it is not my will that you are heavy and unduly full of sorrow. Whatever you do, you will have sorrow. Therefore I want you to understand it is your penance and you will see in truth that all this life is a penance that is for your benefit.' This place is a prison; this life a penance. Yet it is a remedy he wants us to enjoy. For the remedy is that our Lord is with us, keeping and leading us into the fullness of joy.

And this is the endless joy for us that our Lord means, that he will be our bliss when we are there, yet he is our keeper while we are here. Our way and our heaven is true love and sure trust; and he gave this understanding in all, but especially in the showing of his passion where he made me choose him mightily for my heaven.[111]

Flee we to our Lord and we shall be comforted; let us touch him and we will be made clean; cling to him and we will be sure and safe from all manner of peril; for our courteous Lord wills that we be as homely with him as heart may think or soul desire.

But we must take care not to be so familiar that we neglect courtesy. For our Lord himself is sovereign homeliness; yet as homely as he is, so is he courteous, and he is utterly courteous. And his blessed creature that will be in heaven with him without end, he wishes that they be like him in all things. And to be perfectly like our Lord, that is our true salvation and our completed bliss. And if we know not how to do all this, we must beg our Lord to teach us; for it is his own liking and his worship. Blessed may he be!

---

[111] Once again Julian refers to what was clearly one of the most significant lessons of her whole revelation, her determination not to look up to the heaven but stay with her suffering Christ.

78

OUR Lord God in his mercy shows us our sin and our feebleness by his own sweet gracious light; for our sin is so vile and so horrible that out of his courtesy he will not show it to us save in the light of his grace and mercy. And there are four things he wants us to know. The first is that he is our ground in whom we have all our life and our being. The second, that he keeps us mightily and mercifully all the time that we are in sin amongst all our enemies that fall upon us (and we are so much more in peril when we give them occasion and are ignorant of our own need). The third is how courteously he keeps us and makes it known to us when we have gone astray. The fourth is how steadfastly he abides in us, not changing his regard, for he wants only that we turn and be united to him in love just as he is to us. And so by this grievous knowing, we come to see our sin usefully and without despair; for truly we need to see it in this way. And once we have seen it so, we shall be made ashamed of ourselves and be broken from our pride and presumption. For we need to see in truth that of ourselves we are nothing save sin and wretchedness.

And so it is that by the sight of the lesser which our Lord shows us, the greater which we do not see is also laid waste. For in his courtesy he measures the sight for us, for indeed it is so vile and horrible that we could not endure to see it as it really is. And by this humble knowledge, through contrition and grace, we shall be broken from all those things that are not our Lord; and then our blessed Saviour will heal us perfectly and make us one with him.

This breaking and this healing our Lord means in respect of humankind in general. For those who are highest and nearest to God, may see themselves as sinful, and as needy, and with me. And I, who am least and lowest of those that will be saved, I may be comforted with the one that is highest. Thus has our Lord so oned us in charity: when he showed me that I should sin, because of the joy I had in beholding him, I did not attend properly to that showing. But our courteous Lord held back from further teaching until he gave me grace and will to understand. And I was taught here that though we may be lifted up into high contemplation by our Lord's special gift, yet we need in all this to know and keep sight of our sin and weakness. For without such knowledge, we cannot achieve true humility and without that we may not be saved.

I also saw that we may not have this knowledge by ourselves, nor of our spiritual enemies; indeed they wish us no such good, since if they had their way, we would not see it until our dying day. And so we are greatly in God's debt in that he himself wishes, from his love, to show us it in time of mercy and grace.

79

I also had further understanding in this; for when he showed me that I would sin, I took it literally meaning only myself, for I was not moved otherwise at that time. But from the high and gracious comfort of our Lord that followed later, I saw that his meaning was general, that it went for every sinner that ever was and will be unto the last day. Of which I hope in God's mercy I too am a member. For the blessed comfort I saw is large enough for us all.

And here I was taught that I should look only at my own sins and not the sins of others, unless this might be of comfort and help to my fellow Christians. And also in this same showing, when I saw that I would sin, I was taught to be fearful of my own frailty. For I do not know how I shall fall, neither do I know the measure nor the greatness of my sin. I would like to have known this, with due reverence, yet I had no answer.

At the same time, our courteous Lord also showed most surely and mightily the endlessness and the unchangeability of his love; and again, by his great goodness and the inward keeping of his grace, that his love and our soul shall never be parted in two, without end. And so, in this dread, I have matter for meekness that saves me from presumption; and in the blessed showing of love I have matter for true comfort and joy that saved me from despair.

All this homely showing by our courteous Lord, it is a lovely lesson, and his own sweet, gracious teaching to comfort our soul. For he wants us to know, by this his sweet and homely loving, that all we see or feel, within or without, that is contrary to this, is from the enemy and not from God. So that if we find ourselves inclined to be more reckless in our living rather than keeping our hearts because we have known this plentiful love, then we need greatly to beware. For this prompting, if it appears, is untrue and we ought to hate it greatly, for it has no likeness to God's will.

And when we do fall from frailty or through blindness, then our courteous Lord touches us, stirring us, and he calls us by name; and so he wants us to see our wretchedness and meekly acknowledge it. But he does not wish us to linger there, nor does he want us to be busy accusing ourselves, neither does he wish us to remain full of self-loathing. Instead, he wants us to listen carefully to him; he all at the ready[112] and waiting upon us sorrowful and mourning until we come, impatient to have us with him. For we are his joy and delight, and he is our salve and our life. And although I say he stands all alone, I fail to speak of the blessed company of heaven and speak only of his office and his working here on earth, for such was the condition of the showing.

---

[112] *al alufe*: has become 'aloof'. But 'luffed up' was, and is, a nautical term meaning 'directly into the wind', the helmsman waiting the skipper's word for which way next.

80

THERE are three things we stand upon in this life; by these three God is worshipped and we are sped, kept and saved. The first is the use of our common sense;[113] the second is the common teaching of holy Church; the third is the inward gracious working of the Holy Spirit: and these three are of one God.

God is the ground of our kindly reason; and God, the teaching of holy Church; and God is the Holy Spirit. All are different gifts which he wants us to regard and attend to. For they work continually in us and all work us to God: these are great things. Of which great things,[114] he wants us to know here, like some simple ABC: that is to say we have a little knowing now whereof we shall have a fullness in heaven – this much is to speed us.

We know by faith that God alone took our kind, and none but he; and furthermore that Christ alone did all the works that belong to our salvation, and none but he. And right so, he alone now does the last end;[115] that is to say, he dwells here within us and rules us and governs us in this life of ours to bring us to his bliss. I believe and understand the ministration of angels just as scholars tell of, but it was not shown me; for it is himself that is nearest and meekest, highest and lowest, and he does all. And not only all that we need, but he also does all that is worshipful to our joy in heaven.

And where I say he abides mournfully and grieving, it means all those true feelings we have within ourselves of contrition and compassion, and all our mourning and grieving that we are not oned to our Lord. And all such that is helpful, it is Christ

---

[113] *manys reason naturall*: man's natural reason. But what do we mean by common sense except being honest with ourselves?

[114] *that is to seyn*: yet in truth, Julian is frantic to communicate this simple cipher of her experience – we know nothing, yet we will know All.

[115] That is, achieves his purpose and follows through his plan.

in us; and though some of us feel it seldom, it never passes from Christ until such time as he has brought us out of all our woe; for love can never be without pity. And in whatever time we fall into sin and leave him out of our mind and the keeping of our own soul, then Christ alone keeps sole charge of us. It is then that he stands mourning and grieving. Then it is our task from reverence and kindness to turn in haste to our Lord and no longer leave him alone. He is here alone with us all; that is to say, only for us is he here. And all the time I am a stranger to him by sin, despair or sloth, then I let my Lord stand alone, inasmuch as he is in me. And it goes the same way with all us sinners. But though we act like this many times, his goodness never suffers us to be alone; but he is with us lastingly and excuses us tenderly and ever shields us from blame in his sight.

81

OUR good Lord showed himself in various manners, both in heaven and in earth, but I saw him take no other place but in the human soul. He showed himself on earth in the sweet Incarnation and in his blessed passion. And in another manner, he showed himself in earth where I say: 'I saw God in a point.' And in other manner, he showed himself in earth as if in pilgrimage: that is to say, here he is with us, leading us and so he shall be until he has brought us all to his bliss in heaven. He showed himself different times reigning, as I have said before, but principally in the human soul.

There he has taken his resting place and his fair city; out of which worshipful seat he will never rise or remove himself without end. Marvellous and solemn is the place where our Lord dwells. And therefore he wants us to listen readily to his gracious touching, more rejoicing in his whole love than sorrowing in our frequent falls. For it is the most honour we can pay him of all that we might do, that we live gladly and merrily for love of him in our penance. For he beholds us so tenderly that he sees all our living and penance. The natural longing we have for him is ever a lasting penance in us; and this penance is his work in us and mercifully he helps us to bear it.

Because of his love he is always longing, while his wisdom and his truth with his rightfulness makes him suffer in us here; and this is the way he wants it to be in us. For this is our kindly penance and the highest, as I see it, for this penance never leaves us until the time we are fulfilled when we shall come to have him as our reward. And therefore he wants us to set our heart in the overpassing: that it to say from the pain that we now feel into the bliss in which we firmly trust.

82

AND now our courteous Lord showed the meaning of this grieving and mourning: 'I know well that you will live for my love merrily and suffer gladly all the penance that may come to you, but inasmuch as you do not live without sin, for my love you would suffer all the woe, all the tribulation and disease that might come to you. And it is true. But do not be grieved too much by sin that falls to you against your will.'

And here I understood that the lord beholds the servant with pity and not with blame, for this passing[116] life asks not to be lived without all blame and sin. He loves us endlessly, and we sin habitually; and he shows it to us full mildly. Then we sorrow and discreetly mourn, as we turn ourselves towards

---

[116] 'passing': changing and not lasting: but also changing through suffering (passion).

beholding his mercy, as we cleave to his love and goodness, seeing him that is our medicine, and knowing that all we can do is sin. And so by the meekness we get in recognizing our sin, faithfully knowing his everlasting love, thanking and praising him, we come to please him.

'I love you and you love me; and our love shall not be parted in two; and for this gain do I suffer.' And all this was showed in my spiritual understanding with the saying of these blessed words: 'I keep you full surely.'

And by the great desire that I have in our blessed Lord that we shall come to live in this manner, that is to say, in longing and rejoicing, as the whole of this lesson of love shows, I understood from it that all that is contrary to us is not from him, but of enmity. And he wants us to know this by the sweet gracious light of his kind love. And if any such lover there be on earth that is continually kept from falling, I know them not, for it was not shown to me. But this was shown: that in falling and in rising we are always preciously kept in one love. For in the beholding of God we do not fall, in the beholding of ourselves we may not stand; and both these are true, as I see it. But the beholding of our Lord God is the highest truth; and so are we greatly bound to God that he will show us this high truth during our lifetime. And I understood that while we are living here, it is very helpful for us to see both these truths at once; for the higher beholding keeps us in spiritual comfort and true rejoicing in God. And the other, that is the lower beholding, keeps us in fear and makes us ashamed of ourselves. But our good Lord always wants us to direct ourselves much more to beholding the higher, at the same time not leaving off knowing the lower, until such times as we are brought up above; and there we shall have our Lord Jesus to be our reward, for then will we be fulfilled in joy and bliss without end.

83

'Our faith is a light, kindly coming from our endless day,
that is our Father, God; in which light our Mother, Christ, and our good
Lord the Holy Spirit lead us in this passing life.
Our faith is our light in our night; which light is God, our endless day.'

I had in part touching, sight and feeling in three properties of God, in which the strength and effect of all the revelation stands; and these were seen in every showing and most especially in the twelfth, where many times it was said: 'I it am.'

The properties are these: life, love and light. In life is marvellous homeliness; in love there is gentle courtesy; and in light there is endless nature. These three properties were in one goodness; unto this goodness my reason sought to be oned and cleave there with all my might. I beheld with reverent dread, and marvelling highly in the sight, and in the feeling of sweet accord, that our reason is in God, understanding that it is the highest gift we have received, and that it is grounded in kind.

Our faith is a light, kindly coming from our endless day, that is our Father, God; in which light our Mother, Christ, and our good Lord the Holy Spirit lead us in this passing life.

This light is measured discreetly, standing to our needs in the night. The light is the cause of our life, the night is the cause of our pain and of all our woe, in which we deserve reward and thanks from God. For with mercy and grace, we surely know and live in our light, growing in it wisely and mightily. And when our woe ends, suddenly our eyes shall be opened, and in clearest light our sight shall be full; which light is God our Maker and the Holy Spirit in Christ Jesus our Saviour. Thus I saw and understood that our faith is our light in our night; which light is God, our endless day.

84

THE light is charity, and the measuring of this light to us is done for our benefit by the wisdom of God; for neither is the light so large that we may see our blissful day, nor is it hidden from us; but it is just such a light in which we may live with due reward, with deserved toil and endless worship from God. And this was seen in the sixth showing where he said: 'I thank you for your service and your toil.'

And so charity keeps us in faith and in hope; and hope leads us in charity. And at the end all shall be charity. I had three manners of understanding about this light, charity: the first is that charity is unmade; the second is that charity is made; the third is that charity is given. The charity that is unmade is God; charity made is our soul in God; charity given is virtue. And that is a gracious gift of working in which we love God for himself and ourselves in God and all that love God, for God.

85

AND in this sight I marvelled highly; for notwithstanding our simple living and our blindness here, yet endlessly our courteous Lord beholds us in this working, rejoicing. And in all things we can most please him by believing this wisely and truly and by rejoicing with him and in him. For as truly as we will be in the bliss of God, praising and thanking him without end, so also we have truly been in the foresight of God, loved and known in his endless purpose from without beginning. In this unbegun love he made us, and in the same love he keeps us and never suffers us to be hurt so that our bliss could be the less.

And therefore when the doom and judgement is given and we have all been brought up above, then we will see clearly in God those secret things that are hidden from us now. Then will none of us be stirred to say: 'Lord, if only it had been thus, then it had been full well'; but we shall say all with one voice: 'Lord, blessed may you be! For it is thus, it is well. And now we see truly that all thing is done as it was always ordained by you before anything was made.'

86

'Would you know your Lord's meaning in this thing?
Know it well: love was his meaning.
Who showed it you? Love.
What did he show you? Love.
Wherefore did he show it you? For love.'

THIS book is begun by God's gift and his grace, but it is not yet performed, as I see it. For charity pray we all to God, with God's working, thanking, trusting, rejoicing; for so our good Lord would have us pray, such is my understanding that I took in all his own meaning, and in the sweet words where he says full merrily: 'I am the ground of your beseeking'; for truly I saw and understood our Lord's meaning; why he showed it was to have it known more than it is, and in this knowing he will give us grace to love him and to cleave to him. For he beholds his heavenly treasure on earth with such great love that he wants to give us more light and solace in heavenly joy, drawing our hearts from the sorrow and darkness we are in.

And from the time it was shown, I often desired to know what was our Lord's meaning. And fifteen years and more after, I was answered in spiritual understanding, with this saying:

'Would you know your Lord's meaning in this thing? Know it well: love was his meaning. Who showed it you? Love. What did he show you? Love. Wherefore did he show it you? For love. Hold yourself therein and you shall know and learn more in the same; but you will never know nor learn another thing therein without end.'

Thus was I taught that love was our Lord's meaning. And I saw full surely in this and in all, that before God made us he loved us; which love was never slaked, nor never shall be.

And in this love he has done all his work; and in this love he has made all things profitable to us; and in this love our life is everlastingly fixed.

In our making we had beginning, but the love wherein he made us was in him from without beginning; in which love we have our beginning. And all this shall be seen in God without end; which may Jesus grant us.

Amen.

* * *

Thus ends the revelation of love of the blessed Trinity showed by our Saviour Christ Jesus for our endless comfort and solace, and also to rejoice in him in this passing journey of this life. Amen, Jesus, Amen.[117]

* * *

I pray almighty God this book come not but to the hands of them that will be his faithful lovers, and to those that will submit themselves to the faith of holy Church and obey the wholesome understanding and teaching of those that are of virtuous life, serious age and profound learning; for this revelation is high divinity and high wisdom, wherefore it may not dwell with one that is thrall to sin and to the devil. And beware that you take not one thing after your affection and leave another,

---

[117] This and the following paragraph are recognized to have been written by the scribe rather than Julian.

for that is the condition of a heretic. But take everything with the other and truly understand that all is according to holy scripture and grounded in the same, and that Jesus, our very love, light and truth, shall truly show to all clean souls that with meekness ask of him perseverance in this wisdom. And you, to whom this book shall come, thank highly and heartily our Saviour Christ Jesus that he made these showings and revelations for you, and to you, of his endless love, mercy and goodness, for your guidance as well as our own, so as to conduct us to everlasting bliss; which may Jesus grant us. Amen.

Glossary

The words listed below are marked with an asterisk * at their first occurrence in the text.

again-making: the redemptive process, as understood by Julian. She sees it not as a commercial deal struck between God and humankind or between the pleading Christ and his just Father, but rather as the supreme act of love expressed outwardly (so that we experience it) in the Incarnation and Christ's passion. Into this working we come as we realize the Trinity's meaning – of love – and cooperate in the expression of our living.

behold, beholding: Julian's apophatic keyword: not ruminate (rumination) but the contemplation that is the still enjoyment of exchange between God and the soul

beseek, beseeking: seek after, try to get, beg earnestly

blessed (blissid): bringing bliss

bliss: delight, happiness, joy, blesssedness (especially of heaven). As used sometimes the word retains its root meaning of 'that by which means we are blessed': cf. 'the joy and bliss of his passion' (ch. 23).

blissful: (see *bliss*) properly only of the Trinity

buxom (buxum): meek, pleasing, obliging, gracious

courteous: gracious (courtly); in combination with 'homely' it is the special quality that Julian experiences in God's dealings with her, and a defining quality of her message of God's love

disease: discomfort, distress (verb)

dread: fear, trepidation, (as adjective) awe-filled

full: most, very

homely: (adjective) belonging to the home, domestic; hence familiar. It bears the same insight when used in this context as Christ bidding his disciples call his Father, Abba, which they immediately knew as the most familiar address possible.

keep, keeper, keeping: creative property of the Father who endlessly keeps his creation kind: (noun) nature; (adjective) especially belonging to our human nature; but also used of God's nature, that which belongs to God

kindness: the condition of kind, nature; acts which flow from nature, as in ch. 63: 'He feeds us and helps us, according to the high soverign kindness of his Motherhood that answers our kind needs of childhood.'

overpass: (verb) surpass, overcome, cross over, migrate, die

overpassing: (adjective) overflowing, transcendent, excessive (Hilton); (verbal noun) transcendence, death, dying

property: that which belongs in kind to e.g. God or humankind

rightful: right-full: the two words should be dwelt upon literally, as they echo back and forth their conjoining meaning. Julian uses it primarily of God's deliberate, fully wise actions; then in a derivative sense. God himself is rightful: cf. 'this rightful knitting' (ch. 53). All God's acts are perfectly intentioned and fulfilled since he alone is right-full.

sensuality: the sinful side of kind, which is being transformed by the workings of mercy and grace (ch. 55)

speed: prosper, attain one's purpose or desire

speedful: expedient

substance: the ground of our being that is held one in our Maker; Julian sees it as untouched by sin although knitted to our sensuality

sweet: sweet, to be savoured, to be tasted; used of a spiritual salivation that quickens the soul's appetite; especially belonging to the person of Christ

very: true, real or only (Latin verum)

virtue (noun), virtuous (adjective): merit, power; of Christ's acts, especially the passion, applied to working our again-making

weal and woe: good and bad (weal means wealth); Julian experiences the ups and downs of spirit, sometimes quite unconnected with sin

working: (verbal noun) life's task of seeking God, collaborating with him in his again-making process, expecially in the beseeking of prayer

worship: honour, merit (our own: ch. 49)

worshipful: full of honour, honourable, glorious dignified, upright, honest, praiseworthy